PENGUIN

FINDING THE FREEDOM TO GET UNSTUCK
AND BE HAPPIER

Ven. Dr. Douglas Cheolsoeng Gentile, Ph.D., is an award-winning research scientist, educator, and author. Professor Gentile conducts research on the media's impact on children and adults, as well as how mindfulness practices can reduce anxiety and improve happiness. Named as one of America's best 300 professors by the Princeton Review, he is a fellow of several scientific organizations, including the American Psychological Association and the Association for Psychological Science. In addition, Ven. Douglas Cheolsoeng Gentile is a Zen Buddhist monk and meditation teacher. With decades of scientific research and training in several styles of Buddhism under his belt, he has dual expertise in Western psychological science and Eastern philosophy.

He wrote and narrated the best-selling audiobook *Buddhism 101: How to Walk Easily over Rough Ground* and *Meditation: The Busy Person's Guide to Cultivating Compassion and Positive Mind States*. Dr. Gentile has appeared on NPR's *Morning Edition* and the BBC World Service, and his work has been featured on CNN, *Good Morning America*, *The Today Show*, *The New York Times*, *The Washington Post*, *Los Angeles Times*, and hundreds of other media outlets around the world.

Holding a doctorate in child psychology from the Institute of Child Development at the University of Minnesota, Dr. Gentile is the author or editor of several books and well over 140 peer-reviewed scientific studies. He holds a M.Div. from Buddha Dharma University and has also trained at the multi-lineage Interdependence Project in New York City.

Finding the Freedom to Get Unstuck and be Happier

Ven. Dr. Douglas Cheolsoeng Gentile

PENGUIN BOOKS

An imprint of Penguin Random House

PENGUIN BOOKS

USA | Canada | UK | Ireland | Australia
New Zealand | India | South Africa | China | Southeast Asia

Penguin Books is part of the Penguin Random House group of companies
whose addresses can be found at global.penguinrandomhouse.com

Published by Penguin Random House SEA Pte Ltd
9, Changi South Street 3, Level 08-01,
Singapore 486361

First published in Penguin Books by Penguin Random House SEA 2022
Copyright © Ven. Dr. Douglas Cheolsoeng Gentile

ISBN 9789815017137

Typeset in Garamond by MAP Systems, Bangalore, India

www.penguin.sg

This is for Lauren, who told me she wanted me to write books, and for the late Ven. Dr. Wonji Dharma, from whom I still had so much to learn.

Table of Contents

List of Figures

Introduction

This might sound familiar to you—when I was about 19, I was having a highly dramatic and angst-ridden time.

I had finished my first year of college at St. John's College in Annapolis, although 'finished' is probably the wrong word. I wasn't enjoying college, and consequently was not doing well. I was told that I should 'take a year off to see if I might be happier somewhere else.' I didn't know what I wanted to do. I was working at a pizza place, making $2.10 an hour, which barely covered my share of the rent for an apartment I shared with two other people. I was dating a girl, but felt like I should be getting back together with my old girlfriend from high school (always a bad idea). I devised a clever plan to have my best friend present the idea to her (harkening back to the 7th grade, where high romance was defined by passing a note saying, 'Do you like Jimmy? Check this box if *yes*.').

My clever idea worked about as well as you might expect. My best friend spent the evening making out with her. He had the courage to tell me that to my face, and I responded with all the grace of a three-year-old not getting candy for breakfast. I had the strength to maintain this lack of dignity when I met with her the next day, describing my horror and suffering as equal to the Hindenburg disaster, only lacking an announcer punctuating my self-pity with 'Oh, the humanity!'

In the face of this apparently never-ending series of tragedies, I decided to leave society altogether. I went to the army surplus store and purchased a Korean-War-era tent. I gathered some supplies and a thin sleeping bag and determined to walk into the wilderness of Maryland and head up into Pennsylvania, perhaps to arrive at my grandparents' house.

I had no idea how to find a wilderness to walk into, so I asked the woman I was actually dating (as opposed to the one I had wanted to get back together with) to drive me to the outskirts of town so that I might find the wilderness. This would finally prove that I didn't need anyone! I had suffered the slings and arrows of outrageous fortune clearly more than any other person in history, and I was determined to end that suffering by striking out on my own, relying on nothing other than my incomparable wits.

I lasted almost one full day.

The beginning of my epic trek to manliness started well enough. I was dropped off by a lightly wooded area in the late summer afternoon. I hiked along railroad tracks until the sun began to set. I had brought a piece of rope to tie the pieces of canvas together and string them to the nearby trees, and after only an hour, I had managed to make something I could fit inside. I hadn't brought a ground cloth, because I didn't know how tents work. I rolled out my sleeping bag on the plants and sticks, and prayed that I had chosen a plot of ground that no bugs ever visited. Satisfied that my life was finally on track, I turned off the flashlight and tried to go to sleep on the lumpy ground.

I was awakened many times, but what terrified me were the sounds that exist in the night. I am a city boy and had no idea that there are things that move around, chatter, climb, and are curious about tents.

As my terrifying vigil continued, I began to realize that humans apparently need to live in society—that we are social creatures. My desperate struggle against the bloodcurdling sounds of a curious raccoon showed me that being on my own wasn't going to solve my problems, and indeed, seemed to create others. Having heroically survived the night, I set out again. After an epic half-hour of hiking, I came to a road and decided that walking along it would be easier.

By around 9 a.m., I was tired of walking and decided to hitchhike. I sat on the guard rail at a curve on the road, overlooking pleasant, rolling hills. Few cars passed, and none seemed interested in picking me up. In the distance was a church on a hill. By 10 a.m., I was tired of waiting to be picked up and was also starting to feel hungry, having already eaten half of my week's provisions of granola bars. I kept looking at the church and felt like maybe I should go to it. I grew up as a preacher's kid, so I knew that churches tend to be good places to go get free food, or at least to sit inside and avoid the heat.

The church was on the top of a little rise, with a long driveway leading up to it. The driveway continued past the church up another hill to the parsonage. Finding no one around, I sat in the sanctuary and spent more time pondering my place in the universe and digesting the idea that maybe my wandering in the wilderness for almost seventeen whole hours had taught me everything I needed to know about the human condition. After an hour, the minister came in. I asked him if there was any work I could do in exchange for a meal. I spent some time pulling nails out of boards, deciding that I should just call my girlfriend and ask her to pick me up.

As I waited for her to arrive, the minister called me into his office. He was probably about 40, with short hair and a thoughtful demeanour. He asked me to sit, and he told me this story.

'One day, I was working in the church office, and I saw a station wagon drive up. It didn't stop at the church but kept going up the hill to the parsonage, where a man and a woman got out of the car and knocked on the door. Finding no one home, they got back in the car and drove back down to the church as I stood at the door to meet them. I knew what was coming and I dreaded it. Inside the car were the mother, the father, and three small children. They all got out of the car as I opened the church door. The mother saw that there was a water fountain inside and asked if she could take the children in to get some water. When she went inside, the father told me that their grandmother was very sick and they were driving from Atlanta up to York, Pennsylvania to see her before she died. They were very poor and didn't have enough money for gasoline, and could he help them out and give them money?

'Just then, the mother came back out of the church with the children, and I turned to her and asked her where they were going. 'Philadelphia.' Her husband yelled, 'No, no! Don't you remember? We're going to York.' I asked why were they going, and she said 'to see my sick aunt.' Her husband yelled, 'No, it's our grandmother!' By then they had realized that I wasn't buying their story and they piled back in the car and zoomed off.

'I felt terrible for exposing them. I went back inside the church, fell to my knees, and prayed to God that the next time someone comes to me asking for help, they truly need help.'

I stared at him, thinking just how clever he was to have not been tricked. He looked at me like he knew me, and said, 'Thank you for answering my prayer. You were in need, and you were sent here to help restore my trust.'

I was shaken.

Why was I in that exact church at that specific time? Was it karma? Was it fate? Was it, as the minister believed, Divine intervention? Was it just a random series of events? I had made this grand gesture, taken an epic adventure into the wilderness just to try to shake things up in my life, and nothing really seemed different. Humans put themselves in some odd predicaments, and then shout into the wind that it's unfair they're in the situation into which they put themselves. We set ourselves up for suffering, and then seem surprised when we suffer. We make decisions, believing that we have free will, only to realize that we've chosen the thing that keeps us locked into the pattern we were already in. I couldn't answer any of these questions at the age of 19, but they set me on a path of questioning how people make choices and take actions, only to find that they often lead to more problems rather than fewer.

I expect that you have pondered some of these same questions, perhaps wondering why we get stuck in unhealthy patterns. Many people say they keep getting into the same argument, over and over again. It might be with a parent, a spouse, or a child. Some people dread going home for the holidays, 'knowing' that they'll just end up in the same patterns with the same old feelings. If you've ever felt this way, then this book can help you. The science of karma helps us to recognize how we not only are conditioned and controlled by our pasts, but also how we then reinforce exactly the wrong choices and we stay stuck.

I have examined these questions in my practice as a Zen Buddhist monk, which allows me to describe the traditional teachings on liberation from suffering and karmic patterns. You don't need to be a Buddhist to be able to use these ideas to be happier, just as you don't need to be a mathematician to be able to do addition. I have also considered these questions in my professional life as a research psychologist, which means that I can help you understand the science behind karma and free will. Modern psychological and neurological sciences have begun to provide some surprising insights that illuminate the traditional teachings.

Many people I speak to are baffled by why they do things they think will make them happier, only to find out that they're right back where they started. They can often feel the weight of old baggage they still seem to be lugging around. Sometimes it makes them act in ways that seem strange even to them. Perhaps you have felt like this. Do you sometimes feel like you need to try to control the situations and people around you, only to find that you keep setting yourself up for disappointment? Maybe you realize that you have expectations of what others should be like, what your life should be like, or how you feel like you need particular outcomes to be a certain way, only to find that the situations you carefully crafted don't turn out the way you planned. This can make people feel terribly inadequate, which only compels them to try to figure out how to control the future better the next time, which simply continues the cycle of suffering and disappointment.

I assume that you have picked up this book because you are tired of getting stuck. If you keep second-guessing yourself, worrying about past mistakes, future choices, or not being 'good enough,' then this book can help. It takes a lot of bravery to look at yourself clearly and to recognize that maybe you are getting in your own way. It takes even more courage to decide to try to understand why.

Many of us get to a 'line in the sand' moment, where we're finally ready to commit to changing something and then we put in honest and real effort. Perhaps we try to change our diets, exercise differently, try meditation or yoga, or simply be kinder to ourselves. These are valiant efforts and I respect these attempts greatly, but too often they fail to produce the desired effects. Why? It's not because we can't change.

It's because we asked the wrong questions starting from the wrong assumptions.

If you've ever given thought to the topics of karma or free will, I'm going to directly challenge your beliefs. These topics are too often reduced to a sound bite or a bumper sticker, and they aren't what we think they are. I will break them down and show you what they aren't and what they are. It's likely that the beliefs you currently have aren't correct, and frankly, they haven't been serving you or you wouldn't have gotten stuck. Instead, this book will show you where and how karma and free will are active in your life, and this awareness will open up the ability to make them work for you, rather than against you.

In this book, I will introduce you to Diane—not her real name— who got stuck in some very difficult situations and patterns. Like you, she recognized that she needed to do something different. Through an understanding of how karma and free will operated in her life, she was able to get unstuck. I invite you to explore these questions for yourself and find the keys to radical freedom and happiness.

Part 1: Learning Karma

CHAPTER 1:
Understanding Karma Can Help Us Get Unstuck

Diane

Diane was excited and—she had to admit it—a little anxious. In her late 20s, she was finally going back to college. 'I worked in a factory, which was difficult work. I had moved up to the accounting office, which was better; but I wanted to get a degree, so I could get a better job and be happier,' she told me.

Diane was tall and slender, with dark hair and hazel eyes. She had a gentle confidence, and she tended to take things in quietly. Although she was pretty with an engaging smile, she didn't smile often. When she was ten, she had removed one of the hair ties with plastic ball ends from her long hair, absentmindedly put it in her mouth, and pulled at the elastic. When she let go, the plastic ball broke her front teeth, and the paediatric dentist did a bad repair job. As an adult, her teeth looked perfect, but the habit of keeping her mouth closed still clung to her.

It was a bright, late summer afternoon, with the warm sunlight lighting the trees and buildings. 'As I got out of the car, I took a deep breath. Everything felt vibrant and golden. I was excited to be doing something to help myself. My second thought, as I looked around, was how old I felt. There were very few students my age,' she laughed.

Diane had married young, and everything was going well. David, her husband, also worked at the same factory. 'We lived near our families, had a nice house, and were starting to think about having a baby. Everything felt like life was on track.'

How would this one decision to go back to school play out, she wondered? Having some experience in her professional life with both accounting and computers, she took one class in each that first semester. Because she was working, two classes were the most she could take at once.

'I knew it would take a long time to finish, but I knew I was smart enough and I wasn't afraid of hard work. Some of the consequences of going back to college, such as the difficulty of keeping work, family, and school balanced, I expected.' She paused and looked away sadly. 'Some of them, however, I could never have predicted. By the time I realized it, it was too late.'

Trying something new and challenging brought Diane into direct contact with habitual patterns that she and David had created. What should have brought more happiness and freedom created a great deal of stress and suffering instead.

What is Karma?

As Diane will discover, we all get stuck in habitual patterns, sometimes emotional, sometimes behavioural, sometimes relational. These patterns can last for years. Often, by the time we realize we're stuck, we no longer know how to get unstuck.

There is no single, simple definition of either karma or free will, and the oversimplification of them causes problems. Instead, we will examine them in increasing depth. Why is it useful to understand karma and free will correctly? If you misunderstand karma, you're more likely to get stuck. And if you misunderstand free will, you're more likely to stay stuck. With correct understanding, we can gain contentment and ease in times of difficulty, but the real benefits are in what we lose. We lose the constant sense of anxiety, of needing to try to control the uncontrollable. We lose the momentum of our past conditioning and trauma, and begin to see the freedom inherent in each moment.

We want to believe that we are in control of our thoughts, feelings, and especially of our actions. That is, until we do something bad. Then we often want to blame the situation or other people.

Sadly, humans are not good at recognizing where our thoughts, feelings, preferences, opinions, motivations, and actions come from. Some of them come from our evolutionary heritage. Some come from our prior experiences, learning, and conditioning, some from situational influences, some from relational influences, and some are actually from our own free will. We usually can't tell the difference.

For example, we are aware that we like some smells and dislike others. This just seems like common sense and something 'true' about us as individuals. But *why* do we like some smells more than others? One clever study discovered part of the answer.

Several men were asked if they would wear the same T-shirts to bed two nights in a row.[1] After waking up each morning, they put the shirts into a plastic Ziplock bag. Each shirt therefore was infused with the smell of each man, and the researcher collected all the bags of shirts. Forty-nine women came into the lab, and were handed six Ziplock bags of shirts. They were asked to open the bags, take a deep smell of each shirt, and rate how pleasant and sexy each smell was. The ratings were averaged to try to understand what smells were preferred. Surprisingly, no one man's smell was the most preferred by all of the women. But there were strong preferences, and they were very predictable.

All the women and men in the study had their DNA tested. The researchers paid specific attention to a group of genes called the Major Histocompatibility Complex (MHC genes), which are a crucial part of the body's immune response system. Every woman had strong preferences, but they weren't random—women preferred the smells of men whose immune systems were different from their own. From an evolutionary perspective, this is highly adaptive. Your child will have a stronger immune system and be healthier if it inherits different sets of immune genes from each parent, rather than two that are similar. Although predictable, this does not fit with our day-to-day real-world experience. You probably don't notice someone's smell and say, 'Mmmm … your immune genes smell really good today.' Instead, we just know we like some smells and not others, but we do not know why. This can be called **fixed karma**, determined by the actions of others—in this case, your parents. We do not have much control over it, although we can work with it by using perfumes, deodorants, and expensive soaps and shampoos. Nonetheless, our genetic heritage controls what smells we prefer.

We also have **changeable karma**, where we can take actions that will have consequences or lead to different outcomes in the future. Many of the opportunities, problems, and concerns that you have today are due to actions you and others took in the past. As I sit here writing, I chose a specific type of background music, partly because of what I was exposed to as a child. The fact that I can type is due to taking a typing class in high school. The reason I am writing this particular book and not one on how to make erotic balloon animals is because I am trained as both a research psychologist and a Buddhist monk, rather than as a balloon artist. As you can see, we have a lot of ability to shape ourselves and our futures, yet, we often feel stuck in our lives.

When we feel stuck, we might blame our 'karma.' Is this fair? Maybe. Does it mean we are at fault for our situation? Yes, partly. Does it mean that we can't do anything about it? No. Understanding your karma can help to show you how to get unstuck.

What does karma actually mean?

Karma is one of the few Sanskrit words that has been adopted into English without translation. This has led to it being used in ways that are not accurate. It has become a type of chameleon, changing its meaning based on the whims of the person using it. It sometimes becomes a way to blame the victim, such as when we tell people who were abused that it was their 'karma.' It is sometimes used as if there is some type of cosmic scoreboard keeping track of 'good karma' and 'bad karma' points. It is used in ways that make no sense at all, such as on 'My karma ran over your dogma' bumper stickers. Ultimately, it is related to the Sanskrit verb root *kri*, meaning 'to do' or 'to make', and its basic translation is simple: it means 'action'.

The word karma appeared in very early (before 1,500 BCE) Hindu writings, such as the *Rigveda*.[2] In this context, the action was that of ritual actions, such as ritual sacrifices. 'At the dawn of the Brahmanical tradition of India, performing karma was a way of putting things in order. If there was disharmony or conflict, one went to a priest to put things back in order. Harmony was restored this way, and so there was no real moral connotation or dimension attached to it.[3] In this early Vedic sense, then, karma was actions taken in reaction to circumstances. It wasn't particularly personal, as the priest might be using the actions to improve crops, or help reduce diseases.

Within the early Buddhist tradition, it continued to mean action, but in the sense of action and reaction—that our actions have consequences and we can learn from this and use it skilfully. Karma, therefore, became much more personal, where our actions have consequences, specifically for ourselves. This focus on the results of our actions, however, allowed the accumulation of more luggage, such as the concepts of 'good karma' or 'bad karma'. This change allowed it to become used as a foundation for ethical behaviour. As it interacted with cultural and religious beliefs about rebirth in some Hindu and Buddhist cosmologies, it began to take both backward- and forward-looking significance. As some commentators have noted, 'When we try unpacking the connotations the word carries now that it has arrived in everyday usage, we find that most of its luggage has gotten mixed up in transit. In the eyes of most Americans, karma functions like fate—bad fate, at that: an inexplicable, unchangeable force coming out of our past, for which we are somehow vaguely responsible and powerless to fight.'[4]

Misunderstanding karma can have important, and potentially devastating, consequences. Some people blame others for things that are clearly not their fault; for instance, saying that early childhood trauma was 'just your karma.' Others treat karma like some type of magical bank account that allows us to hoard our 'good' karma for a rainy day. Buddha was very clear that his teachings had only one goal—to liberate people from their suffering. Both of these examples oppose the basic Buddhist goal of liberation, and are, therefore, unskilful approaches to working with karma.

There are additional ways karma is misunderstood and used as a bludgeon, creating more suffering rather than less. It is often used when bad things occur, leading to the idea of karmic 'retribution,' where the universe somehow has to balance out good things with bad, or where a punishment is always lurking around the corner if you ever make a mistake.

One student of mine stated, 'I have found myself using expressions pertaining to good or bad karma, mostly in high school. When my friends or I would do something good, we would rack up "good karma points" or say things like "she will get her bad karma." I have since stopped using such phrases because I understand now that the world is not a just place.' This is a typical misunderstanding, resting on the assumption that karma is a force that is somehow trying to keep balance at a personal level—by punishing transgressions and rewarding good behaviours. For those of us raised in the West, this is a very typical approach to understanding religious teachings—we will be judged for our actions. Karma in this conception is, therefore, highly related to ethics, but it acts on them from the outside the same way the fear of imprisonment may keep someone from committing a crime.

Karma can also be misunderstood as a type of predestination, leaving people to wonder what place free will has. If our current situation was determined by karma, and every action will result in some corresponding consequence, then where is free will?

There are answers to these questions; answers that can help us to live with a greater sense of freedom and joy. Karma and free will are not what we think they are. Modern, scientific psychology has yielded some dramatic new insights about free will.

Developing a Pronoid Mind

My definition of an enlightened being is one who trusts that the next moment will be workable. She/He is not anxious about what might happen, nor ruminating over past errors and injuries. This person feels a sense of calm even when life's turbulence is roiling. This person can act with true free will—aware of, but not controlled by the impulses and feelings that come from our past conditioning. Because the enlightened being trusts the next moment, she feels a sense of balance. Balance is not a singular stable place, but a dynamic centre that allows an action to emanate in any direction. Much of the time we find that we are leaning in one direction, preferring a specific outcome. That makes it difficult to go 'with the flow,' because we are already off balance, leaning one particular way. When we are truly balanced, we are equally able to move in any direction in reaction to the demands of the situation. This is another aspect of free will. Free will isn't simply getting what you want—it's being free to go in any direction. When we are balanced at the centre of the chaos that life presents, we not only stop feeling victimized by it, we become more available to others, and more able to engage fully and deeply with our lives.

This deep trust in the next moment may sound difficult to achieve, but it shouldn't be. In fact, it has been the truth of almost your entire experience on earth. Our real-world experience can be summed up this way (it's an oversimplification, of course, but it is nonetheless generally accurate): Every moment of your life, the universe has given you enough.

Take ten minutes and contemplate all of the millions (literally!) of things that have to keep going exactly right for you to stay alive one more minute. Some of these are at a microscopic level, such as your body continuing to break down proteins and amino acids in just the right way, your immune cells dealing with all of the parasites you come into contact with, and the bacteria with whom you are symbiotic maintaining the correct balance with your digestive tract cells. Some of these are at an interpersonal level, such as no one shooting you or running their car over you, and others growing and processing food for you to be able to eat. Some of these are at an environmental level, such as having sufficient oxygen, water, heat, and not too many pollutants. Some are at a cosmic level, such as the sun continuing to shine and the earth continuing to turn. The literal truth is that millions of things must go exactly right for you to live one more minute. The odds of all of these things continuing to be just right seem astronomical, and yet, your entire real-world experience is that all of your life, they have. It's as if the universe is conspiring to make you happy!

Unfortunately, we spend much of our time feeling anxious and upset. Why? Every moment is giving you exactly enough. It might not be what you want, you might not be enjoying it, you might be in pain, but it is still enough and always has been. Rather than trusting our own experience, we become paranoid—worried about what was, what is, and what might be.

The word paranoid has Greek roots. *Para* means 'around, against, contrary to, irregular, or issuing from'. *Noid*—a form of *nous*—means 'mind'. Thus, we generate a mind that is contrary to reality, that is irregular, wanders around, and creates an alternate version of reality. What if we worked to generate a frame of mind that is *pronoid* rather than paranoid? *Pro*—from Latin—means 'before, forward, taking care of, just as, or favouring'. Thus, a pronoid mind would be one that is forward thinking, looks forward, takes care of us, and sees something just as it is.

The universe, and almost everything in it, is conspiring to make you happy. It is doing it very sneakily, so we don't usually see it, but that just means that the conspiracy is wide and deep. How can we learn to abide in this pronoid mindset? There are several methods.

A method you can use right now is to meditate on a koan by 9th century Chinese Zen master, Linji (Jp. Rinzai; a koan is a Zen teaching statement or story). Take a stable seat, where you are not rigid, but are nonetheless holding yourself up (note the inherent meaning in this posture). After settling into your breath for a couple of minutes, bring to mind this question and try to answer it in as many ways or as much detail as you can. 'What, in this moment, is lacking?' Spend ten to twenty minutes on this question for a few days, and you may be surprised to find that you can relax your paranoid and anxious mind.

As we learn to trust that we can work with what arises, we gain some clarity and space to see our karmic momentum—the pushes and pulls of our past conditioning that maintain our reactive and anxious minds. This is a first step toward getting unstuck.

CHAPTER 2:
The Ripples in Our Lives

Diane

Having left her job at the factory, Diane took a job as the personal assistant to Karen, one of the co-owners of a small financial services company. Karen was one of those people who attracts talent by being warm and open, and deeply interested in everyone around her. She had Italian roots, and maintained a friendly focus on food and family, often inviting the company employees to her house for excellent dinners.

The office was stylishly furnished and open. Various toys like a unicycle and balls to throw were strewn about the office to stimulate creativity and create a fun atmosphere. Karen appeared to be an excellent person to work for, caring about each of her co-workers individually. This was until it became clear that Karen had a pattern — she had one employee who was her favourite and one who was the 'bad' employee. By chastising one and praising another in view of the full office, the dynamic among the employees changed. Within weeks, what had been a wonderful job became anxiety-producing. Diane felt a subtle competition to become the favourite, or at least not to be the bad child.

Diane was the favourite for a while, which felt wonderful, but also stressful, because it was clear that the position was tenuous. 'When you were the favourite, Karen would bring you flowers, coffee, or gifts for no reason. She would stop and talk to you and give you anything you needed,' Diane said with a faint smile. 'If you did something she didn't like, however, she would completely ignore you and not answer your emails or questions. It was never clear what made someone the favourite, so we never knew what to do. It was like working for dysfunctional parents. It created a toxic atmosphere every day.'

It is likely that Karen believed she was just giving honest feedback to help individual employees. Nonetheless, an action directed at one person influenced everyone—having a 'favourite' made everyone tense.

The ripples of this one action extended far beyond what Karen expected.

Karma of Result and of Cause

Ripples in a pond are a great example of how karma works in the world: the difference between the two types of karma: the karma of result and the karma of cause[5], sometimes referred to as old and new karma.

The **karma of result**, or old karma, recognizes that the present circumstances of our lives are the results of actions performed at some previous time. For example, I am a father now because of actions taken many years ago. These actions do not necessarily have to be 'ours,' but include other actions, causes, and conditions that have influenced us and our actions. For example, I couldn't have become a father all by myself. Everything that we are at this moment, our habits, our personalities, the opportunities we have, and the situations we find ourselves in, are the result of prior actions.

In contrast to this, the **karma of cause**, or new karma, recognizes that the actions we perform at this moment condition our futures. I sometimes think of this using a water drop metaphor (Figure 1).

When we take some action, it makes ripples that extend outward from it. The ripples can be shallow or deep, depending on the strength of the action we took. It is likely that you have done something in your life that hurt someone else, and the ripples extended beyond the person you had hurt directly to other people who were connected to both you and your victim—this would be similar to a dropping a large rock in the water. To take an extreme example, when I was in high school, one of my classmates murdered another student. This obviously affected both

Figure 1: Our actions (karma) send ripples outward. (Photo by Terry Vlisidis
on Unsplash)

the victim's and perpetrator's families. The students and the teachers
were distressed. The perpetrator shot the victim six times early in the
morning, and then came to school and sat next to me. I'm still weirded
out by how totally normal he seemed that day. My brother Bobby was on
the football team with the victim, and this devastated the team. Because
the shooter was white and the victim was black, racial tensions flared
up. Protests and fights began to break out both in school and in the
community. Police had to patrol the school hallways because the tension
was so high. Although it was a private action between only two people,
the effect was felt by hundreds of people, and I'm sure some people still
feel it deeply to this day.

One problem with the stone in the water analogy is that it is fairly
static, suggesting we stay at the centre of the ripples. It would be a
better analogy if we added motion. For example, consider that we're
in a boat, moving in a direction that could catch up with some of the
ripples. If we have done something that made a large ripple (e.g., we
hurt someone), the ripple moves outward, but we also continue moving
away from the origin of the ripple. As we move forward, our boat

catches up with the ripples and starts to rock as it feels the effects of the ripples we made.

Let's take the relationships at Diane's workplace as an example. When her boss Karen showered one employee with praise and favours, it usually had the desired effect of making that employee happy to have been recognized. The ripple did not stop there, however. Other employees noticed the exuberant praise and attention. Some of them felt jealous because they had previously been the favourite and now weren't. Some felt anxious, worrying about whether Karen would now be even more critical of them and their work. Some realized that they were never likely to be the favourite and withdrew even more. I'm certain that Karen did not realize that by making one employee temporarily happy, it made most of the others enjoy working for her less. Over time the 'favourite' mantle was passed on to another employee, the negative feelings grew. Within a year, most of the employees had left.

When they quit, Karen's boat caught up to the ripples she had previously created and now the boat was rocking perilously. When an employee leaves, it is difficult for a small business as they need to find someone new, but still have to get all the work done while they are conducting the search for the candidate. This couldn't have been what Karen had wanted. She honestly seemed to like her employees and thought they helped her business. It would have been much more efficient and much less emotionally difficult—for her and everyone else—if she had just treated everyone benignly. Then, she wouldn't be stressed and stuck doing everything herself because so many people quit.

At this point of high stress—which was so bad that it put her in the hospital—all she could see was the ripple she was now experiencing. She blamed all her employees for being bad employees and leaving her. She never saw that the ripple was of her own making. Had she seen that, she would still have to deal with the situation as it is, the karma of result, the effects of her earlier actions; but she would have had a chance to change her leadership behaviours to change future ripples, the karma of cause.

Our Actions Interact with Others'

A second limitation of the ripple analogy is that it focuses only on our own actions and ignores the fact that we are interconnected with many other beings, all of whom are also making their own ripples in the pond we're moving through (Figure 2).

We, therefore, not only feel the effects of the ripples we make, but we can also feel the effects of those that others make. When a busy street is closed, it changes traffic patterns on other streets, affecting many people . When a business lays off workers, the whole community can feel the effects of that. The remaining employees

Figure 2: Everyone else is making ripples too.
(Photo by Isi Martínez on Unsplash)

may worry that they are next. The local economy can become depressed. When a terror attack happens somewhere in the country, we all feel it. The ripples of the attack on September 11, 2001 are still being felt by the families who were directly involved, by businesses that were destroyed, by public perception of Muslim people, and by government policies.

This rather simplistic way of viewing karma demonstrates two things. First, we are the inheritors of not only our own karma, but also the karma of others—we are all in the same pond. Therefore, our karma is individual, relational, and communal, all at once. Second, this analogy can help us see the interaction that exists between the karma of result and the karma of cause. The ripples we're feeling today are due to actions that we previously performed, the prior actions of others, and the direction we are going in. From where we are at this moment, however, we could always change direction and could take actions that will lessen or enhance the ripples around us.

We've all been in situations like this. Sometimes we're the rock. Sometimes we're the ripple. Sometimes we are riding the ripples of others' rocks, just as they must ride ours. For example, I once approached a friend about a mistake I felt she had made, and I handled it badly. I thought talking to her separately from her family would be kind, that it could be handled privately. Instead, she felt like I had ambushed her by taking her away from her support system. Several months later, when I tried to interact with her, she was not receptive to me because she was still bothered by my clumsy handling of the prior situation. In addition, it limited my ability to interact with others in her family, even though I hadn't done anything to upset them directly. Thus, the ripples extended out both in time and breadth, and I ended up feeling the reactions to my original action. I didn't anticipate the effects would be so long-lasting or would influence others beyond the two of us. I was disappointed, of course, but this is the karma of result; actions have consequences, and I had to work with them, regardless of whether I liked them or not. Recognizing this allowed me to take actions to heal the relationships, using the karma of cause to take actions intentionally to change the future.

Ripple Contemplations

Take a couple of minutes to think of something that is currently difficult in your life. Maybe you keep having the same argument over and over again with a partner, parent, or child. Maybe there's a friendship that feels strained right now. Maybe you don't feel like you are living up to the goals you had set for yourself. Pick any issue that feels frustrating, difficult, or where you feel stuck. Now, reflect back to an earlier time in that situation or relationship. What actions did you take (or not take) in the past that might be part of why you are feeling the ripple you are in right now? Did you throw a big rock at some point in the past? Or did you just drop lots of little ones along the way that somehow combined to make what feels like a big wave?

It is very difficult to perceive the world from someone else's point of view, because all we have direct access to is our own point of view, and we have practised it our whole lives. Nonetheless, I give you permission to pretend that you are someone else with a different history and a different set of emotional triggers. It might help to consider if you were someone you know pretty well, like a sibling or a close friend. What are a couple of things that this pretend you might have done differently in the past? If you had done those things, can you estimate how things might have changed? Usually it's not a huge change, but still one that would make your current ripple feel different if you had tried doing or saying those things in the past.

Now, consider a time when someone felt angry at you or hurt by you. Perhaps, at the time you didn't think you had done anything 'wrong.' Perhaps, you knew what you did, and you were sorry for it. Perhaps you knew what you did, but you felt justified and believed you would do it again. Regardless of what you believe about yourself and the situation, you threw some rock into the pond and the ripple extended outwards and shook the other person.

Again, imagine yourself to be someone not hampered by your point of view, your pressures, and your motivations. How could this pretend you have done things differently to make the rock smaller? What if you had thrown a second rock after the first, to try to change and ameliorate the ripple pattern? How might that have changed the reaction you got from the person who was hurt and angry? What could you do *now* to change the effect of that original rock?

Being able to evaluate ourselves honestly like this is the beginning of being able to surf on the waves, rather than being swamped by them.

CHAPTER 3: Planting Seeds

Fixed and Variable Karma

As has been noted, karma is not one thing, and there are more ways to consider it than simply the karma of result and the karma of cause. Another useful approach is to compare fixed with variable karma.[6] **Fixed karma** is that which is generally immutable, such as our genetics. I was born male and grew up in America. These are not things I can change, but they both influenced the types of experiences and opportunities I have had. I will be male and culturally American until I die.

In contrast, variable karma is that which I can change with my own effort. The Soto Zen teacher Roshi Yasutani describes it thus: 'Consider the matter of health. A person may be born sickly, but by watching his health can become strong. Similarly, a healthy person who neglects himself can become weak. Longevity is a matter of both fixed and variable karma, fixed because limited by our genetic inheritance, variable because it is also affected by one's honesty and good will'.[7] To illustrate this, the most typical Buddhist metaphor for karma is a seed.

The Bactrian Greek King Milinda, in approximately the 1st century BCE, asked the monk Nagasena, 'Why are men not alike, some short-lived and some long; some sick, others healthy; some ugly and some handsome; some weak and some powerful? Why are certain men poor and others rich; some base and others noble; some stupid and some clever?'

The Elder replied, 'Your majesty, why are plants not alike, some astringent, some salty, some pungent, some sour, and some sweet?'

'I suppose, Venerable Sir, because they come from different sorts of seeds.'

'That is how it is with men too, your Majesty. They are not alike because their karmas are not alike. As Buddha said, "Each being has its own karma. Each is born through karma, becomes a member of a tribe or family through karma. Each is subject to karma—it is karma that separates the high from the low."'[8]

This simple analogy hides great complexity. A seed doesn't necessarily grow into anything. It has to be planted in the right kind of environment. It needs to be in the right kind of soil, get the right amount of sun, get sufficient moisture, planted at the right depth, planted at the right time of year in an acceptable climate, and so on. Even if the seed is planted with the greatest of care, its germination still cannot be accurately predicted, nor can we predict how large or strong the resulting plant might be from that seed. Thus, karma is not a 'law' in the sense of other types of physical laws, such as what goes up must come down.

Recall that Diane went back to college in her late 20s. She had been valedictorian in her high school, and after a year of college, realized she didn't want to continue studying what she had always thought she would like. 'College is a weird time,' she confided in me. 'It's almost like it sets you up for failure. You take 18-year-olds, who have no real-world experience, and give them all this freedom. I learned a lot of things the first time I went to college. I learned that boys are fun. Drinking is fun. Parties are fun. All the freedom to not study is fun. I made a lot of bad choices ... I didn't study like I should have, and I failed chemistry.' She smiled ruefully. 'Okay, fair enough. That was my karma—my actions and the reactions that were a result of those actions. I accept responsibility for it and can work with where things are now.'

No single thing caused Diane to drop out of college at age nineteen. She planted lots of seeds in lots of directions. She studied in some classes and did well in those. She didn't in others, and did poorly as a result. She began dating and learned a lot about herself. She began to see that some things were fixed and some were variable. She had a limited amount of time each day (fixed karma), but she could choose how to use it (variable karma). She was intelligent enough (semi-fixed), but she wasn't applying it (variable). She was female and liked dating boys (fixed), but which boys (variable)?

It might be tempting to assume that karma can be defined as commensurate with Newton's third law: for every action there is an equal and opposite reaction. Diane didn't study and she failed. If you run a red light, someone will cut you off later. If you lie today, you will be lied to tomorrow. Nonetheless, karmic reactions need not be equal or opposite, as they will interact with other actions, causes, and conditions. The Tibetan Buddhist teacher Traleg Kyabgon notes that the idea of karma being a *law* is 'purely a western invention, as there is no such phrase in Tibetan, Sanskrit, Chinese, or Japanese'.[9] A karmic seed has a potential to ripen into an effect, but when or how it does so relies on multiple, related causes and conditions.

Six Conditions of a Karmic Seed

The Yogacara school of Buddhism notes that the operation of karmic seeds is governed by six conditions.[10]

1. Momentariness. Seeds arise, change, and cease without interruption. If seeds were unchanging or eternal, then they could not cause anything in the future.
2. Simultaneity of seeds with their results. Cause and effect are interconnected. The oak tree exists within the acorn and is not separate from it.
3. Seeds function in tandem with the appropriate consciousness, meaning that there is a continuity between the initial planting of a seed and its eventual result.

4. Seeds have the same karmic quality as their manifestations. Wholesome actions produce wholesome seeds, which produce wholesome results (as do unwholesome or neutral actions).
5. Dependency on multiple interconnected causes. Seeds only produce their particular manifestations when the necessary associated causes and conditions are present.
6. Particularity. A seed produces its own particular manifestation and no other. Similar to how different seeds grow different trees, seeds of mental phenomena produce psychological results, whereas seeds of material phenomena produce results of form.

This tradition claims that all karmic seeds are said to have these six characteristics, and if they do not, they are not karmic seeds.

A couple of years ago, a friend of mine from Denmark was going through a difficult time. He was depressed and wasn't able to shake it off. It was having a major impact on his work. I invited him to come and stay with me for a while. This would get him out of his current environment and shake up his habits a bit. It seemed like it might help him. It did. Let's examine it through the six conditions of seeds framework.

1. Everything changes. Depression isn't a single monolithic thing, although it often feels that way. My intention to support my friend is momentary as well. I could have stopped caring at any moment, or given up, or done something to make things worse for him. It is useful to keep re-engaging with the intention to help—to keep the seed alive and nourished.
2. The intention to help is already helpful. We don't need to wait to see the result to know if an attitude of kindness and compassion 'worked.' Having it means it is working already. The end of the path is already at the beginning of the path, otherwise there would be no path.
3. My intention to be of help set conditions for how I thought, felt, and acted. It couldn't force him to be one way or another.
4. My intention was compassionate, which is typically thought of as a wholesome intention. It should therefore bear wholesome fruit.

5. Regardless of my intention, if he didn't engage it couldn't have helped. If he hadn't been able to stay with me, it wouldn't have worked. If the depression was deeper than it was, it might not have worked. If his plane had crashed on the way here, if something else went wrong in his life, if he resented my interfering, and so on …. my helpful intention wouldn't have been able to support his working on his depression and finding a path out. Hundreds of tiny details had to come together to be able to support him, not simply the seed of my intention. Had any one of those other supporting causes and conditions not occurred, the outcome would have been different in some way.

6. My intention was a seed of caring. It could only grow into caring. It could not change him, nor could it change his circumstances. It could only support him as he worked to change.

Dangerous Oversimplifications of Karma

Although the analogy of reaping the results of the seeds we sow is useful, it is easy to oversimplify the karmic process to be one of blame or of some cosmic bank account of retribution. This potentially dangerous oversimplification shows up on the cover of Buddhist magazines with headlines like *Karma & Trauma: 'Is It Really My Fault?'* (*Lion's Roar*, March 2017). It also shows up in writings in multiple Buddhist traditions.

The Tibetan monk Patrül Rinpoche stated, 'If you are falsely accused and criticized now, it is the effect of your having told lies in the past.'[11]

The Theravadin monk Nyanatiloka Mahathera agrees with this view, saying, 'According to Buddhism it is, of course, quite true that anybody who suffers bodily, suffers for his past or present bad deeds.'[12]

Zen priest Philip Kapleau wrote:

A person who accepted karma (i.e., the law of causation on the moral plane) would never be impelled to ask such questions. When tragedy struck him the question would not be *why*, but *how*. 'How can I rid myself of the "bad" karma which brought this about and create "good" karma in the future which will benefit myself and others?' One who truly understood that whatever we reap was once sown by use would inevitably say, 'I don't know why this has happened, but since it has, I must have deserved it.'[13]

This strikes me as an incorrect and potentially damaging oversimplification. When a drunk driver crashes into you, it is not only your actions that you must deal with, but also those of the drunk driver. You can be subject to other people's actions, not only your own. This simple fact is often overlooked. We will discuss this aspect more when we examine relational karma. It is interesting, however, that even Buddha himself did not claim that everything you experience is caused by your previous actions.[14]

We cannot know all of the reasons why things happen. Even when we know something about the seeds that preceded the fruit, the seed alone is never sufficient. It fits within a complex web of interconnected causes and conditions, and everything has to come together for the seed to take hold, sprout, and bear fruit. We cannot know or control all of those aspects, but we can try to be aware of what seeds we're planting with our thoughts, words, and deeds. When we repeat the story of how we are a victim, we keep replanting and fertilizing those seeds. When we are stuck in a bad situation, we can examine some of the seeds we planted that got us here, and then consider how we can dig them up or plant new ones to help change the situation. In this way, we can work with the fluidity of our variable karma.

CHAPTER 4: Karma *is* Learning. Learning *is* Karma.

A Modern View of Karma

Karma is not fate or destiny. Neither is it a type of bank account where we hoard 'good' karma points or spend 'bad' karma. It is much more simple—it is how our learning and conditioning from the past influences the present, and how our present learning can influence the future. The first time we have an experience, we have the opportunity to approach it openly and with curiosity, as a fresh and unknown experience. For example, if you have never heard of the Southeast Asian fruit durian, you may be surprised and intrigued by its hard and spiky exterior, the soft creamy interior, its powerful smell (it's often not allowed on public transportation), and its oddly complex flavour. People tend to have a strong reaction to it, positively or negatively. For some, such as myself, it smells like a combination of sewage, skunk, and old socks, although many others find the smell to be sweet. To me, it tastes like smoky sweet scallions, with a texture like custard. The smell and taste linger for hours. I know several people who love this. I am not among them.

The first time I tried it, I approached it with curiosity and care, not sure what I was experiencing. I didn't really like it, and I found that I really disliked having the smell and flavour clinging to me for the rest of the day. Even a shower didn't fully eradicate the smell. The second time I tried it, I was not nearly as open to it, and was much less curious. I have had many more opportunities to have durian. I no longer take them. This is not good or bad, but it demonstrates an important aspect of individual karma—that we learn from our experiences and that learning can colour and change our future experiences. Learning is probably the best modern synonym for karma—we come into a new situation thinking we already know or expect something because of past experiences we've had.

Learning is such a natural set of processes that we often do not realize how effortlessly we learn. Humans and many other species have multiple, different learning mechanisms, so just saying 'learning' doesn't make the meaning clear. This is not the place for a discussion of all learning mechanisms, but it is worth considering a few of them in detail to see how learning is a type of karma.[15]

Diane

After Diane dropped out of college at age nineteen, she moved back home and started dating David, a tall and good-looking man she had known from high school, back when she was a freshman and he was a senior. By her late 20s, she had been married for years, had a house, a job, was on her way to having her first child, and was feeling like it was time to begin growing again. Taking classes at the local community college reignited her love of learning.

'Everything in my life felt great,' she told me. 'I wasn't running away. I just knew I hadn't been living up to my potential and now that everything was on track, I could begin growing and learning again. I still had this nagging feeling that I 'should' get some sort of degree, if for no other reason than it would help me get better jobs. I knew I was smart enough, and didn't want to only be able to search for entry level, no education required types of jobs.' She paused while she remembered that time in her life. 'My jobs had given me some experience with accounting and computer support, so I took a class in each. I got all As, which I felt great about after not being in school for so long. I was ready for this again.'

She smiled and stirred her coffee. 'Everything seemed so clear right away. I hated, hated, hated accounting. I loved programming. I really understood the languages, the logic, how it all connected. So I took as many classes along that path as I could. Because I was working and had a family, I could only take one or two classes a semester, but it was very rewarding to feel competent at learning something new.'

She took a sip of her coffee and I sensed her mood darken. 'It didn't last. My husband David started complaining about my taking classes. He couldn't see the value in education, and he took it all very personally. I couldn't take pride in what I was learning because he criticized me for it. He made fun of me for wanting to read or study instead of just watching TV. He complained that I wasn't at home when he wanted, that he had to watch our daughter, or if he had to make his own dinner. He complained that it was taking so long. I didn't understand. Here I was doing something that was not just good for me, but would be good for our family, and he kept attacking me for it. I was hurt that he didn't have any interest in what I was doing.'

She sighed. 'Each new class, he would say that I was just trying to get away from him. If the class was useful for my intellectual development but not directly related to computers, he'd really get angry about it. 'What does learning Japanese have to do with computers?' he'd yell. I couldn't even talk to him about his concerns, because once he had expressed his dislike, he would stop talking to me for about a week.'

'Wow, really? He would punish you by refusing to talk to you?' I asked. 'That's really cruel. How did you handle it?'

'He would go into other rooms to avoid me, or if we had to be in the same room, he'd have a scowl and pointedly not look at me. I had to walk on eggshells until he decided it was okay again by some metric I never understood. It could last from two to ten days, and when he felt he was done not talking, he'd act like it never happened. I constantly felt like I wasn't good enough. Not a good enough wife. Not a good enough mother. Not a good enough student. If I had been good enough, I should have been able to make all these things work together.'

'I had felt really good about taking classes and learning and growing. Now it made me feel sick to my stomach. I got depressed. Finally, after about three years, I just quit taking classes because it was easier. But that really made me feel like I wasn't good enough. I had dropped out of college at age nineteen and now again at thirty-one. I started to doubt everything about myself. Maybe I wasn't as smart as I believed. Maybe I was too selfish and should stop trying to grow, like David said. I couldn't see the point if there wasn't anyone to care or support it.'

Learning Type 1: Operant Conditioning

Remember that one of the ways karma acts is by changing our responses to our current situation based on the conditioning we've had in the past. Diane's story shows one main way we learn and are controlled by our past learning—through rewards and punishments. When she failed (a punishment) in college when she was nineteen years old, it changed her whole trajectory. She had planned to become a pharmacist, but failing chemistry sent her back to her home town. Having someone show interest and attraction (reinforcement or reward) led to marriage. Getting good grades when returning to school (reinforcement) validated her and made her want to continue growing. Having her husband punish her for taking classes made her quit. Now, when she thought about a new class, she couldn't see it as it was—just a class. Instead, the thought of class made her depressed and anxious because it suggested conflict and disapproval. This is karma—not being able to relate to the current situation directly and honestly for what it is, but having it be coloured by past learning.

What happened *after* Diane took the action of going back to school changed and controlled her future in some way. In psychology, this is called operant conditioning. In the course of a day, we try various behaviours, often to achieve some desired consequence or goal, such as taking a class.[16] What matters for learning is what happens *after* the behaviour. Studying can lead to a good grade, which makes one want to continue studying. Getting punished for taking the class can make one want to quit. At a technical level, the organism learns to control its environment while simultaneously being shaped by the environmental consequences.[17] When this occurs, we say that the behaviour has been reinforced, meaning that the probability of the behaviour occurring again in situations that seem similar goes up.

Reinforcement can occur in two ways. Positive reinforcement occurs by gaining something desirable, as when working earns money, or when one clears a level of a video game and gets access to new levels or skills in the game. Negative reinforcement occurs by escaping or avoiding some negative outcome or noxious stimulus, such as when a dog jumps a barrier to escape a punishment, or a student studies hard (or maybe cheats) to escape a failing grade. Notice that positive and negative do not refer to good or bad behaviour: whining can earn attention and cheating can earn a high grade.

Voluntary behaviour can also be modified via extinction and punishment. Extinction is the process of non-reinforcement, which teaches the learner that responding in previously rewarded ways is no longer effective. Thus, the behaviour eventually decreases in frequency, although not smoothly because non-reinforcement is frustrating, and the behaviour has not been forgotten. Punishment, in contrast, provides an aversive consequence to the behaviour, such as David's criticizing Diane's taking classes. Punishment can also be positive, where something unpleasant is gained (like getting a speeding ticket), or negative, where something desired is taken away (losing your driver's license). The usual effect of punishment is that the behaviour is suppressed, at least momentarily in the presence of the punisher (consider speeding when police are present). Many complexities and side effects accompany extinction and punishment, including frustration effects,[18] learned helplessness,[19] and masochistic behaviours.[20]

Operant conditioning is analogous to Darwin's natural selection: behaviours survive and are maintained because the consequences selected them. At a simplistic level, if you go to a new restaurant and have a great meal, the odds of you returning go up. The behaviour (going to that restaurant) continues to happen in the future, because you were reinforced last time. If, instead, you get food poisoning, the odds of you returning go down. The behaviour (going to that restaurant) stops and never happens again in the future, because you were punished last time. The consequences of a behaviour, therefore, are primary in conditioning future behaviour and the frequency of the continued behaviour. Nevertheless, behaviours occur in a situation or context that provides cues for appropriate behaviour. Red and green traffic lights cue our stop-and-go behaviours; they do not force us to stop. Rather, we learn to discriminate when it is appropriate to stop or go, presumably because of the consequences associated with those behaviours. Once learned, the cue signals the appropriate behaviour, and over time, this can become habitual, requiring little conscious control.

Even more important than the amount of reinforcement is the schedule of reinforcement—that is, whether it is reliable and consistent or variable and intermittent. It may surprise you to learn that the best way to get behaviours to last is through intermittent reinforcement.[21] If you know that you will always win a game, it gets boring and we soon stop playing. It's the not knowing when we might win that keeps us playing, that's why people will lose for a long time at slot machines in the hope of one win. This can also work with punishments—Diane never knew when David might choose to show his disapproval by ignoring her, so she became constantly anxious.

The reason I am spending so much time talking about how humans learn is because our learning controls us (and remember that I am suggesting that learning *is* a type of karma). Once we've learned something, we don't usually even notice having learned it—we just act differently and it feels natural to us. If we do notice that we're stuck, or that we keep getting into the same situations over and over again, or that we're doing things that aren't helping us, we often don't know why. If we can see the ways we've learned, and how it has been reinforced and punished, we can then start to get unstuck as we are not simply being controlled by our prior conditioning anymore. If we never learn to notice our learning, however, it is much harder to break free of negative patterns or to gain more positive patterns. Learning to notice our learning and karma is made more difficult, however, because humans learn in many different ways. Operant conditioning is only one of several learning mechanisms. Let's talk about a few more.

Learning Types 2 & 3: Habituation and Sensitization

I once worked in a company where the main group of employees all had known each other prior to working together there. When I began my job there, I was shocked to see that my colleagues all treated each other like they were at a band camp. They spoke sarcastically to each other and made fun of each other as a way of trying to be fun and friendly. To me, however, it felt very disrespectful. Nonetheless, over time I started getting used to it and no longer noticed it. That is, until a colleague of mine visited the office and pointed out that it felt like a very hostile work environment, with everyone seemingly mocking each other all the time.

This demonstrates another type of learning—*Habituation*—a decreased responsiveness to something. Repeatedly show a baby a picture of a person and measure the amount of time the baby looks at it. On as few as three presentations, the baby's time attending to the picture will begin to decrease. This is evidence of learning: the baby can recognize that picture.[22] If I were to show you a horror film and measure your heart rate and blood pressure, they would probably go up. If I showed you the same film again, your heart rate would go up again, but less than before. If I show it to you repeatedly, after some time you would stop reacting to it, you'd be bored. Boredom in this case is evidence of habituation, despite the fact that you were not trying to learn the plot. All that is needed for habituation is repeated exposure to a stimulus. In fact, even a single exposure that is too fast to be consciously noticed can be learned and can change one's behaviour.[23]

Habituation also explains our ability to learn to tolerate unpleasant or threatening situations, such as the example above where my co-workers made fun of each other. Enter a space with a strange smell and it will immediately be noticeable, even jarring. Remain there for some time and you will get accustomed to the smell. The smell could be increased gradually over time and we would adjust to it and show greater tolerance of it. Thus, like the proverbial frog that would jump out of hot water, but will tolerate slowly warmed water that eventually exceeds the temperature of the initial hot water, we learn to tolerate that which was previously intolerable. This is part of the reason why we may stay in unhealthy relationships—we lose the ability to see how we are harmed because we become habituated. It also helps to explain why we may not see the warning signs in the next relationship. Karma is not a mystical force—it is simply how our prior actions and learning influence our perception, attitudes, and actions in the present.

We have many different learning mechanisms, and some of them appear to complement or oppose each other. Returning to my workplace, I became used to the atmosphere of everyone teasing each other. I recognized that they were using sarcasm as a way to show their trust and closeness. Over time, I not only became habituated to it, I felt like I should join in the allegedly friendly banter. This posed a problem for me, however. I don't really like sarcasm as a form of humour—it has an edge that can cut the other person. It feels dangerous in that if you poke just a little too hard or in the wrong direction, you can really hurt the other person. You've probably had the experience of someone going just a little too far and it harmed your relationship for a while.

Instead of sarcasm, I prefer flirty humour and innuendo. Rather than putting down another person, this can show that you appreciate the other person and also show a level of trust and closeness. This backfired big time. My sense of humour was outside of the group norm, and offended some of the team. In response, I got sent to hours of harassment training. What the training did was to make me very careful about the way I spoke in the office. This is a different type of learning, where we become *more* sensitive to something in the environment, called *sensitization* in psychology. Again, this is just a natural way humans learn, and it is a way karma manifests. For example, it is like post-traumatic stress disorder, where we become hyper-sensitive to some cues in the environment because they remind us of something we had serious difficulty with. We can no longer interact with those things openly as they are because they remind us too much of something we were harmed by. As Diane's husband complained and punished her for taking college classes, she became sensitized to his moods. She talked about 'walking on eggshells,' which is being hypersensitive to any cues that may point to his withdrawal of his attention and love again. To put it in terms of karma, when she was leaving class, she would begin to feel anxious on the drive home, worried about whether he would be warm or cold to her when she walked through the door. Her conditioning changed her experience of her life. At this time, she couldn't just drive and enjoy the drive. She couldn't just walk through the door and see what was happening. She couldn't be open to what actually was, because her karma/learning was colouring all of her experiences, thoughts, and feelings.

Learning Type 4: Classical Conditioning

Another learning mechanism humans share with many other species is called classical conditioning, where we learn to pair certain types of things together. When I was three years old, my father was in the army. I have very few memories of the time, but one incident influenced me for almost twenty years. It was time for me to get a vaccine, and my mother did not want me to be scared. She told me that if I didn't cry I would get a lollipop. Unfortunately, she took me to the army nurse on the base. The nurse treated me like one of the recruits. She lifted the needle in the air, and then quickly jabbed it into my leg harshly. I didn't cry. I screamed! If I recall correctly, I got TWO lollipops, because my mother knew how much it had hurt.

How is this a story about learning or karma? From that point onward, I was terrified of needles. Any time I needed to get a shot or a blood test, I would clench up involuntarily. Of course, clenching up only made the shot hurt much more, which further reinforced my fear of needles. Even twenty years later, when I actually knew that clenching made it worse, I couldn't stop myself. This one painful event coloured all of my later experiences and made them more painful than they would have been if I could have approached each one like a new experience.

When two things happen together, we can learn to connect them even when they aren't truly linked. If one of them is a biological reflex, such as fear in response to pain, we can learn to have the same reflexive response to cues associated with it, in this example, the sight of a nurse. This is the learning mechanism known as classical conditioning. You probably know the classic Pavlov's dog study, where the sound of a bell conditioned dogs to salivate at the anticipation of food.[24] Once learned, the reaction to an eliciting stimulus is involuntary and may not even be recognized by the person.

Pavlov's contemporary, John Watson, also studied how reflexes can be conditioned and aimed to catalogue which habits or reflexes could be considered 'natural' and which should be considered 'learned.'[25] In 1920, he provided the classic demonstration of conditioned fear in what is known as the Little Albert study. This experiment is problematic and could not be conducted today, but is important in the history of learning psychology. Little Albert was an approximately 9-month-old baby who was found to be a remarkably calm and curious baby. When suddenly shown 'a white rat, a rabbit, a dog, a monkey, [people wearing] masks with and without hair, cotton wool, burning newspapers, etc.' He showed no evidence of fear (Figure 3).[26]

During the training phase, at about eleven months of age, Watson put the white rat in front of Albert and an unseen person hit a steel bar with a hammer, causing a sudden, loud noise. As with almost all babies, the loud noise scared Albert and he began to cry. After just a couple more times of putting out the white rat and making the sound, Albert began to fear the white rat and would cry and try to get away from it even though there was no loud sound (Figure 4).

Although this is interesting by itself, what was really surprising is that now that Albert had learned to fear the white rat, he also was scared of many other things that he previously had not feared. These included a brown rat (perhaps not too surprising), a white rabbit (more surprising), a brown rabbit (much less like a white rat), a medium-sized brown dog (not at all like a white rat), a Santa Claus beard, and so on (Figure 5).

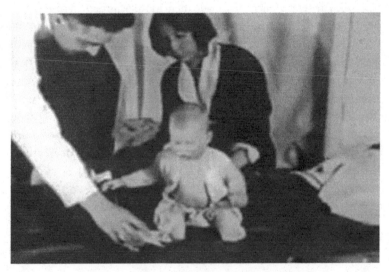

Figure 3: Albert, prior to conditioning, shows no fear
Source: www.chronicle.com

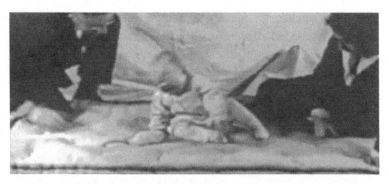

Figure 4: After conditioning, Albert now fears the white rat.
Source: www.macleans.ca

Figure 5: Albert generalizes his conditioned fear to be afraid of things not very
similar to a white rat
Source: Wikimedia Commons

We will return to the story of Little Albert later, but to clarify how
learning happened here, the noise triggered fear and crying—this was an
unlearned, reflexive reaction to a sudden loud noise. There happened to
be a rat nearby at the time of the sound, and the fear became connected

to the sight of the rat, despite there being no real connection between the rat and the sound. Albert learned to fear the rat because it was paired with something that instinctively scared him, but he then generalized that learning to other things that had not been paired with the noise.

Despite the apparent ease with which classical conditioning can occur, there are significant limits. Generalization to other stimuli goes only so far. Fear of a white rat generalized to other furry objects, but not to a wooden duck.[27] Animals made sick by a blue liquid will avoid other liquids with the same taste or odour, but they will not associate the nausea with blueness.[28] The principle here seems to be that we are biologically prepared to associate tastes or odours to food, and fears to sounds or appearances. Still, conditioned emotions are one important level of learning, which interacts with behaviour and cognition. This is perhaps one of the most important ways our karma (learning) works. We bring a conditioned feeling into a new situation, thus preventing us from being completely open to the situation.

My colleague Patrick told me about a supervisor he once had who was critical in a way that seemed unfair to him. 'She would ask me to write a report, and no matter what I did, it was always too late and wrong. I became paranoid—is it just me, or is she like this with everyone? It was always "red alert." There was no sensible way to work and no rational discussion. She wanted the results to be different from what they were, no matter how it was done. I started doing everything I could to avoid her. I turned down interesting projects and tried to work entirely on my own.

'On the one hand this worked well. I reduced my daily stress because I didn't have to see her or worry about how she might react to something I did. On the other hand, however, it hurt my career. I didn't get to do work that would have been useful for me. I didn't get my name on papers that were important.'

I asked him whether he had ever been able to approach a meeting with her openly, rather than defensively, to see if she acted differently. 'No, I just always assumed she would be the same, so I was defensive even before I walked into the room for a meeting.' He paused and leaned back thoughtfully. 'I honestly don't know if she might have been different if I could have approached her differently. I got so anxious just thinking about her that I always withdrew and was defensive.'

This is one example of how emotional conditioning (karma) can work. If we've had a bad experience with a person in the past, we feel some of those feelings the next time we have to be with that person. This colours our perceptions, judgments, and actions. Even if the other person comes to the next situation in a gracious and kind mood, we are likely to act in a way that impels that person to be difficult again, and the cycle is reinforced one more time. Note that this is not necessarily bad. There is a real wisdom in learning from our experiences, and if someone has acted abusively toward us in the past, it is wise to be sensitive to this in our following encounters.

Learning Type 5: Observational Learning

The human brain is so well tuned to learning that we can learn simply from seeing others speak and act. Imagine yourself as a young child, about kindergarten age, and your mother or father bringing you to a new place. Perhaps you're a little scared because you have never been there before and you don't know what to expect. I give you some crayons and a paper, and let you entertain yourself for a while. This is fun, and you relax. After a while, I say you can watch a little TV, and turn it on. You like TV, so you turn to watch. On the screen, you see a woman come into a room where there is an inflated clown doll. She goes up to the doll and starts punching it, kicking it, picking it up, throwing it, and sitting on it and punching it. As she does these things, she says certain phrases, like 'Pow! Right in the nose!' After the show, I take you to a new room where there are lots of varied play materials. There is a tether-ball hanging from the ceiling, there is a play stove with pots and pans, there are dolls and balls, a toy gun, and several other attractive toys, including an inflated clown doll like the one you saw on TV. You are told you may play with anything you want to and are left alone to play. What will you do?

If you're like most children, and it doesn't matter a lot if you are a boy or girl, you will copy some of the behaviours you saw on TV. You punch, kick, throw, and beat the clown doll, saying exactly the same things the woman on TV said. This is perhaps surprising, because there was no reinforcement or punishment. Reinforcement is sufficient, but not necessary, for learning. Rather than *causing* learning, reinforcements and other consequences select and shape behaviours, regulating the probability with which they occur.

Now, imagine that you saw the same TV show, but it had something extra at the end. After the woman performed all the aggressive acts toward the doll, a man comes into the room and he either reinforces her behaviours, saying things like 'That looks like a lot of fun. Great job!' or he punishes her for it, saying things like, 'Hey, don't do that. That's bad!' What would happen now, when you are left in the room with all the toys? Again, assuming you're like most children, if you saw the man praise the woman, you will copy many of the aggressive behaviours towards the doll. If, instead, you saw the man reprimand the woman, you won't copy the aggressive behaviours, or at least, you won't do as many of them. Does this mean that you didn't learn them when the woman was punished? No. If I say I'll give you a piece of candy if you show me what you saw on the TV, you can still perform all of the aggressive acts and say the aggressive phrases. So you learned them just as well, but you also learned that maybe you shouldn't do them.

This is essentially what happened in a series of clever experiments by psychologist Albert Bandura.[29] He realized that learning can occur even when it is not observed in behaviour, and even when the learner doesn't realize that they're learning. None of these children were trying to learn. They were just watching TV. They not only learned from seeing the model's behaviour, they also learned from whether the model was reinforced or punished. Children did not spontaneously imitate the punished acts; they did imitate the rewarded acts. The punished behaviours had been learned however, because the children were able to demonstrate them later when asked. Thus, reinforcing or punishing primarily affects performance, not learning. We learn just by seeing, but we also learn to expect whether we might get rewarded or punished if we copy what we've seen. The distinction between learning and performance is important, because we often don't realize we've learned anything until a later experience reminds us of it in some way. This 'reminding' does not need to be conscious to influence our feelings and behaviours, however. For example, a person who has had no real-world experience with Muslim Americans may feel anxious when seeing them at a store or on the street. Why? Because television in America disproportionately talks about Muslims only when linking this beautiful religion with terrorism. In this case, our karma comes from observational learning without trying to learn—from watching television shows and the news, our feelings and behaviours are influenced in a situation they shouldn't be. More disturbingly, when this happens to us, we won't even be aware of it or why we are feeling the way we are.

Learning Type 6: Cognitive Learning

You are reading now. It's just little squiggles on a page, and yet by looking at them, hearing the sounds they represent, you are able to learn novel ideas or to connect ideas in new ways. This is a type of cognitive learning, where we learn by associating cognitive concepts together, by creating new mental representations of concepts, by creating cognitive maps of spatial arrangements, etc. This type of learning also does not require you to act, it just needs you to hear, see, or think something.

We learn by reading, hearing, experiencing, or even thinking something once. When we hear it a second time, it gets relearned and becomes harder to forget. If we repeat it enough times, it can become automatic and habitual. This is why the stories we tell ourselves matter so much. If we constantly repeat that we are 'broken,' we are learning and reinforcing this idea to the point that it will likely never be forgotten. When we try to become unbroken, it can feel almost impossible because we have repeated the opposite way of thinking so much. I've heard it said, although I am unconvinced there is good science behind this, that about 90 per cent of the thoughts you have today, you also had yesterday. If this is even partly true, we should be a bit more careful with our minds.

This is also why the media and news we consume can have a profound influence on us without our conscious awareness. The ideas we generate or come into contact with do not need to be reinforced to be learned, although reinforcement can make learning occur faster.

Ultimately, all of these ideas become 'yours,' and you probably won't be able to recall where you heard them first, or how you came to the conclusions you have. Many of the ideas, beliefs, and attitudes you have also include an emotional component, which will be the final learning mechanism we'll consider.

Learning Type 7: Emotional Learning

Recall the story of Diane earlier in this chapter, who had been trying to go back to school but her husband's dismay derailed her. There was more at play here than simple reinforcements and punishments. There was a strong emotional component to the situation. Her initial failure in college made her doubt herself and retreat from more school for a decade. Her feelings of having a loving family and stable career allowed her to overcome the doubt to begin taking classes again. Her husband's withdrawing his attention and support made her doubt herself again, and ultimately quit classes. Over fifteen years later, she has still not gone back to get a degree. Emotions, especially strong emotions, have a significant effect on learning and how we are shaped and controlled by our past learning.

Emotional learning and memory are related to cognitive learning and memory, albeit distinct forms of learning and memory. The brain has circuits, such as the amygdala, designed specifically to attend to the emotional aspects of situations. These brain circuits support our feelings and expressions of emotions, our learning about the emotional aspects of experiences, and can also change what is learned. There are three major outputs of the amygdala. For example, in response to seeing a car crash, it sends signals three ways. One signals the cerebral cortex so that we become consciously aware of our feelings. A second pathway travels to memory systems (e.g., striatum and hippocampus), which influence attention and therefore what is learned. A third pathway controls our bodily responses, such as hormone release and the autonomic nervous system (the 'fight or flight' response). One important implication is that emotion plays an important role in attention and motivation to attend. Specifically, it moderates attention and memories, and facilitates memory of emotional aspects of experiences and concepts. That is, when we have an emotional reaction, we narrow our focus to pay attention differently, and our brains get ready to remember better at the same time that we are becoming aware of the emotional feeling.

In addition, when we experience an emotional response—especially when the hormones epinephrine and cortisol are released—memory is enhanced. For example, in one study, participants viewed clips from documentary-style films. They viewed both emotionally arousing clips, such as animal mutilations, and emotionally neutral film clips, such as a travelogue. The amygdala and related areas were more active during the arousing film clips, and memory for those clips was better three weeks later than for the neutral film clips. Memory performance was significantly related to the amount of amygdala activation for the emotionally arousing film clips, but not for the neutral film clips.[30]

As we try to understand ourselves, our patterns, where we are free, and where we are stuck, it is useful to examine how our emotions were conditioned and how they subtly influence us to make certain behaviours more available and others seem impossible. These feelings are not usually correct. Almost nothing is impossible, but our past experiences and their lingering feelings make us forget that.

Learning and Karma

Now that we have discussed several learning mechanisms, what exactly am I trying to say? How are they related to karma and to the pursuit of a happier life? I argue that the modern synonym for karma is learning. The actions, thoughts, and feelings we express have consequences, and we learn and are shaped by those actions, thoughts, and consequences. Humans are such natural learners that we usually don't even realize that we're learning. Although we can 'try' to learn, it also happens without our trying, and it happens at many levels. We become habituated, sensitized, and desensitized to things we see repeatedly. We learn when two things occur together, even if they don't have anything to do with each other. We learn simply from trying things and having pleasant or unpleasant consequences. We learn ideas, either from other people, the media, or simply from our own thinking. We learn emotional responses from our own experience and from seeing others' emotional reactions.

We learn to pair emotions with other ideas. All of these can happen independently, sequentially, or simultaneously.

Once we have learned something, however, it usually changes how we approach similar situations, events or encounters in the future. What 'similar' means, however, is surprisingly difficult to define. One would never have guessed that Little Albert would be afraid of rabbits or dogs after being trained to fear a rat. The trepidation with which he now approaches new rats, rabbits, or dogs is a manifestation of karma. Because of past experience, Albert is conditioned to be less open to and more fearful of new experiences with different animals. Notice also that the example of Little Albert demonstrates how the karmic reaction is not necessarily equal nor opposite. In fact, the reaction seems much stronger and broader than it should be to the simple action of hearing a loud sound a few times. Similarly, despite Diane's love of learning, the unpleasant experiences with David kept her from ever getting a college degree. Our learning and conditioning from the past influence the present, and our present learning can influence the future. Although this can be detrimental, it is also good. It means that freedom is possible, once we understand, recognize, and change our behaviours. Even deep emotional baggage can be worked with so that it no longer controls us and our relationships.

Part 2: Achieving Clarity

CHAPTER 5: Starting to Recognize What We Can Work With

Consider the situation you're in at this moment. Perhaps you're reading in bed, in which case you can't hit someone with your car. Perhaps you're listening to this book in your car, in which case you really shouldn't go to sleep because then you'd probably hit someone with your car. The situation you find yourself in has various potentials for action, specific environmental affordances and not different ones, and the recent history and karmic momentum of the situation. This is the karma of result, which can feel like fate. Because of actions taken, both by you and by others, and myriad interconnected past causes and conditions, you now find yourself in a situation where some types of actions are possible and others are not. For example, if you are driving your car on a busy street and it looks like someone is about to run a red light and hit you, you are in this situation because of many reasons, including, but not limited to:

- You got in the car earlier this day and started to drive.
- Many years ago, you learned to drive.
- You have the resources (due to many other previous actions you've taken) to have access to a car (not to mention the innumerable things that had to happen for cars to be created and available at this point in time).
- You took various actions to get to this particular intersection at this time.
- The other drivers all also took various actions to get to this particular intersection.

- The government used tax dollars (some might have been from you) to create roads that exist in this spatial layout.

If you can, take ten or twenty minutes to brainstorm all of the things that had to happen to get you to the place where you are at this precise moment. You will find that there are literally millions of things that had to come together to make this moment possible for you. These include biological functions, genetics, prior generations, the sun continuing to shine, there being enough oxygen, and all of the choices you and others have made over many years.

If you prefer, take some time to consider your relationship with a close friend. How did you two meet? What had to have happened for you both to be able to meet in that way? What actions made the friendship difficult for a while, and what forces have kept you continuing to be friends? Notice that karma—actions and their consequent reactions— are always at play. What tiny change would have made everything different? Notice that you can see some of the ripples from different actions. Perhaps some of these ripples were large and rocked your friendship hard for a while. Some of them might have been actions you or your friend took or failed to take, and some might have been actions from other people that still rocked your world and your friendship. Slight changes can have significant outcomes. It makes me grateful when I look back at all the tiny little things that nonetheless yielded significant results. It sometimes feels like some relationships were destined by the stars. Yet this is not the same as fate or destiny in most conceptions of those concepts.

Fate or destiny suggest that an action must result in a specific consequence. This idea only makes sense if actions work independently of each other and their contexts. Karma, however, works within a network of other causes and conditions that are all functioning simultaneously. Even in over-simplified terms, it has primary and secondary parts:

Regardless of the effect, there is always a primary and a secondary or contributing cause. Consider a bean plant. Seeds are the primary cause of its existence, but to grow, these seeds require soil, water, and sunlight. Had the bean seeds been kept in their dried condition they would not have sprouted, flowered, nor produced new beans no matter how many years elapsed. What was required were secondary causes, in this case soil, water, and the light of the sun.[31]

To come back to the example of being in your car, at that moment, only certain actions are possible. You cannot go sky-diving or swimming at that precise moment, you can only drive your car. You could get lost in thought, or sing along with the radio, or pay attention to the other cars, but you cannot still be in bed. The set of actions you and others have taken recently and in the past have brought you to this moment that touches reality at a very particular place with very particular opportunities for action. This is the outer situation you're in and part of, and there's nothing you can do about what got you to this place. It is as it must be.

Our minds are the corresponding internal side of the equation. How do we perceive the situation, what are we primed to pay attention to, and what various actions might we take? We usually do not have all the possible actions available to us, because of our past learning and conditioning. Humans learn through multiple mechanisms, and this learned information and behaviour can influence how we see the world, what we notice, what we believe, and how we act.

Imagine you come into a room for an experiment and I ask you to put on headphones. I tell you that we're testing how well people can hear through different headphones, and that you are going to hear a someone reading aloud, and your job is just to listen. You listen carefully, but there is a trick. Unknown to you, the sentences don't have all the sounds recorded correctly. For example, four of the sentences have a phoneme missing at the beginning of a word, so what you actually hear for each of the four sentences is the sound 'eel'. The sentences you hear are (1) the *eel was on the axle, (2) the *eel was on the shoe, (3) the *eel was on the orange, and (4) the *eel was on the table. When I ask you what you heard, you never say the word 'eel' despite hearing it four times. Instead, you report hearing the *wheel* was on the axle, the *heel* was on the shoe, the *peel* was on the orange, and the *meal* was on the table. You might not think you would do this, but if you have any prior knowledge about wheels and axels, shoes with heels, orange peels, and meals on tables, then you will perceive these sentences incorrectly (and this is, in fact, what is found when these studies are conducted[32]). In psychology, this is called top-down processing, where we interpret whatever we encounter in terms of what we already know. It is another manifestation of karma, of how our past learning influences our present experience.

Prior learning or conditioning influencing present and future perception and behaviour is not limited to conceptual knowledge, but influences feelings, reactions, tendencies, preferences, etc. I learned this in my own experience when I was about twenty.

'Would you please light the candles on the dining room table?' asked my grandmother. I was visiting during a holiday from college, and although it seemed like a simple request, I felt a surge of anxiety rush through me. I fumbled with the book of matches, tentatively pulling out one. I turned the book over, bent the cover backwards, and tried to pinch the match between the lighting strip and the cover. I pulled the match out, smoking, but not lit.

I tried to calm myself down. What was the big deal? I took a deep breath. The warm smell of my grandmother's Italian sausage and peppers came out of the kitchen, mixing with the dark smell of old coal that still permeated their Pennsylvania row house. My grandmother, whom I called Mam, came into the room and looked at me sadly. 'I know why you're scared,' she said as she sat down.

'No, no, I'm not scared. I just never liked matches. I'm no good at lighting them,' I quickly replied.

'That's not really true, now, is it?'

'What do you mean?'

Mam pulled a chair out and sat down, motioning for me to do the same. The dark wood panelling of the dining room made the crown of white hair surrounding her compassionate face stand out. 'Do you remember when you lived in Rockville, Maryland, when you were four or five?'

I thought about it. I had a vague memory of an ice cream shop that my parents would take me to, and an even vaguer memory of getting the scar on my forehead from one of the older kids golfing a dog bone into my skull. 'Not really,' I answered. 'Why?'

'When you were four, some of the bigger kids in the neighbourhood pressured you to steal matches out of the house and take them behind the garage and light them. Apparently, you did this a lot before your father found out about it. We came down to visit for your fifth birthday, but instead of having a nice party, your father had you out on the back porch. You were standing in front of the grill with a box of a thousand matchsticks, and he was forcing you to light all of them. You were crying because you kept burning your fingers. I was inside crying just as hard as you were.'

She took a deep breath and reached over to hold my hand. 'So that's why you're scared of matches. I'm surprised you don't remember it.'

Mind blown.

I thought I had just never liked matches.

To my father's credit, he used a specific operant learning technique on me called 'implosion,' which is designed to stop a behaviour immediately. He couldn't take a chance that I might continue lighting matches, as the next one I lit might set the house on fire and kill us. It worked. I never touched another matchbox until I was a teenager, and even then, I was super careful and anxious about them. This is one of the ways karma operates—we have an experience, especially an emotional experience, and it colours all of our future experiences that have a similar feature of some sort. Often we may not have any memory of the original experience. We just feel a certain way—we like some things, we don't like other things, we're attracted to this type of person, we're anxious about this type of situation, and we never wonder *why* we feel these. We just think our feeling is how we are and have always been. We believe it's some kind of truth about us, and we never realize that we're being controlled by our past conditioning. This demonstrates to me how a given situation can influence future reactions to situations, even if we have no recollection of the original experience that conditioned us. Any person who has had serious trauma or Post-Traumatic Stress Disorder knows how even a single past experience can have a strong effect far into the future.

Our past conditions our present, and our present conditions our future. I think there are two important messages I learned from this. First, most or maybe almost all of our likes, dislikes, preferences, attitudes, and judgments have been shaped by forces outside of our memories. We had some experience that we liked or disliked, and that shaped the way we perceive and experience anything that seems similar enough to us. Therefore, we should be much more sceptical of our own opinions—they aren't really 'ours' and they certainly aren't the truth. Second, this is a hopeful teaching. Our present experience will be biased by our prior conditioning, but once we recognize that we can take some control over our present and change our futures. Once I knew why I was so scared of matches, the fear lost some of its power. I no longer believed that matches were inherently scary. I was still careful, but realized that I could have new experiences that undermined the prior fear, and within just a year or two, no longer felt any anxiety about matches.

In this example, the effects continued to be specific to matches and did not generalize to other types of fire, but this is not always the case. As described in the last chapter, in Little Albert's case, the effect generalized to a wide range of furry things. Many cases of PTSD are especially difficult to treat because there are a wide range of situations, noises, and sights that can trigger a reaction that is not appropriate for the current situation. Recall from Chapter 3 that one of the traditional teachings about a karmic seed is that it should result in a specific type of result and no other. I now disagree with this traditional teaching. The idea that karmic actions plant seeds that can only grow into something that is of like type[33] seems to be too limiting. Prior learning and conditioning can generalize and transfer to new situations, which is why we often feel stuck. We get stuck in the same types of responses, having the same arguments over and over, ending up making the same types of mistakes even though each new situation is not exactly like the past one. This is funny, because if we asked ourselves whether we wanted to keep staying stuck, we would likely say, 'No, of course not!' And yet, we keep doing the same dumb things. Why is that? Because learning is easy, but unlearning is difficult.

To return to the example of driving the car, your prior experiences in a car will shape the odds of what you are paying attention to, how quick your reflexes are, and what actions you might think to take. If you have practised texting and driving a lot, the odds that you'll be easily distracted and not paying attention to other cars in other directions are pretty high, at least compared to the odds if you usually practise 360-degree awareness and looking far down the road. If you have practised getting in and out of spins, you might try turning the wheel hard to avoid the collision, but if you haven't, you are probably more likely to just step on the brakes. That is, what you have practiced in the past changes the odds of what you're likely to be aware of and the range of actions that you would be likely to take. In other words, we aren't *destined* to act in a certain way in a certain situation, but we certainly become predisposed to pay attention to only particular things and to behave in particular ways based on what we have practised in the past. This is our old friend the availability heuristic—what options appear to us, especially when we are under stress, are limited to those that are most easily available to our minds, and the options that are most available are the ones we've practised the most in the past. This suggests that, perhaps, we don't have total free will, because not all choices are open to us based on what we have practised in the past.

At any given moment, we are in a particular situation and state of mind because of myriad causes and conditions that happened in the past. These past causes limit our possible responses to the situation. If we don't recognize this, we are likely to waste energy trying to do or change something that is impossible in the current situation. Once we do recognize why we're in the situation and the state we're in, however, we can begin to work much more skilfully with what is possible, and this can completely change our futures.

CHAPTER 6: Planting Seeds that Bear Fruit, or, How to Change the Future

Any given situation has specific affordances for behaviour. This is the outer aspect of the present moment. The state that we are in, what we're open to, what we've learned previously, and what we've practiced shape the odds that we might behave in a certain way given the situation are the inner aspect of the present moment. The actions we take can shape future moments. The Tibetan teacher Chögyam Trungpa Rinpoche noted, 'We are here because of our past karmic situation. But what we are going to do, being here, is up to us.'[34]

If our futures were governed by fate or destiny, then our choices and actions would not matter. This concept has a long tradition in Western religious thought. In Greek myths, the Moirai were the goddesses of fate.[35] Moirai means 'shares,' so the Moirai spun out a length of the thread of life at birth, and everyone got their share. It was fixed at birth and directed both your actions and the consequences of those actions. Although Zeus could intervene and change your fate, you yourself had little control over it. In the Iliad, for example, Homer writes of Hera, queen of the gods, saying, 'For all of us have come down from Olympus to take our part in this battle, so nothing may be done to him [Achilles] by the Trojans on this day. Afterwards, he shall suffer such things as Destiny wove with the strand of his birth that day he was born to his mother.'[36] Thus, even with the gods intervening, they could only hold off Achilles' fate for a day.[37] Stupid ankle.

In contrast, the Buddhist conception[i] is that although our current situation is the result of past karma and is therefore unchangeable because it is past, our actions now can definitely change the future. This is the value in understanding karma. Everything that occurs has a cause, including our happiness or unhappiness. Therefore, we can work with our difficulties to gain liberation from our negative patterns and suffering. If happiness had no identifiable causes, then everything would be random and we could not create happiness or reduce suffering.

We have a radical freedom in the present moment as long as we can be aware of our prior conditioning and habits. Unfortunately, we are usually not aware of our habit energy, and so do not take advantage of this freedom. We instead continue to do the same things we typically do, which keeps us locked into the patterns we've already established.

If we return to the metaphor that our actions create ripples that extend outward into the future, and that we will often catch up with them, we can begin to recognize that we have several responsibilities. First, as Chögyam Trungpa said, 'Our responsibility is to relate with things as they are, simply and directly … A synopsis of past history is contained in the present situation, and one proceeds from there.'[38] When we spend time wishing things were different, or wondering why we are in this position, we are wasting energy. If we spend our effort worrying about how we got here, being upset about the past, or worrying about the future, we will have very little beneficial effect on the future because we are putting our energy into places that make no ripples.

The second responsibility, therefore, is to recognize that every one of our actions in this moment matters. Taking no action is still an action that can have consequences. Thus, the Buddhist path is one of great responsibility. 'The Sixth Patriarch of Zen said, 'When others are wrong, I am in the wrong. When I have done wrong, I alone am to blame.' Such a deep sense of personal responsibility could come only from one who truly understood the law of causation [karma], who knew that the network of interrelationships between all forms of life is so vast and complex that we cannot disavow responsibility for whatever happens anywhere, least of all for the repercussions on other lives of

---

[i] At the relative truth level

our thoughts and actions.'[39] Once we recognize that we are not in control of anything, and that every action can create ripples that affect others and our futures, then we become meticulous with our thoughts, words, and deeds.

The idea of destiny is tricky to give up. We might believe that we have freedom to act in this moment, but that once we take an action, the repercussions from that action are fixed. This is not correct in the Buddhist approach to karma. To completely plant a karmic seed that is likely to ripen in the future (again, depending on other internal and external causes and conditions), there are at least four internal factors that influence how well it is planted.[40] These are intention, planning, action, and non-remorse. Every one of these stages is something we can have some control over, once we know to pay attention to them.

Step 1: Intention

It is sometimes said that intention is 90 per cent of karma. If we do an action with no intention, it does not have the same karmic force that it does with intention. It still can have repercussions, but they are not likely to be as severe as if there was intention. In the United States, intention is the primary difference between first-degree murder and manslaughter. In both cases, you have killed someone, but the punishments are much higher if you intended to commit the act than if it was an accident from negligence.

Theravadin monk Nārada Mahāthera expresses this point (and perhaps goes a little too far) when he states, 'Involuntary, unintentional or unconscious actions, though technically deeds, do not constitute kamma, because volition, the most important factor in determining kamma, is absent.'[41] This view may be too extreme. An unconscious action often is a habitual action, and at the very least, repeating it increases the odds of continuing to repeat it. Therefore, even if the unintentional action has no external karmic consequences, it is reinforcing the habit one more time—burning it a little deeper into your brain. Nonetheless, unintentional actions can still have serious external consequences, even if they are not as severe as when they are intended.

Consider David's complaining about Diane's going back to college. From my outside perspective, I don't know all the details, but I doubt he had the intention of hurting her. I think his intention was to exert control, to try to manage her time and attention, which ended up hurting her. What if his intention had been financial rather than to control? If he had complained that they couldn't afford it, would she have been as hurt? Would she have felt unsupported? Would she have felt so much like 'not a good wife?' I doubt it. The direct result of his complaints might have been identical—she quit going. But by having an underlying intention to control, it radically changed the outcome.

Intentions are not something we usually pay attention to, as they underlie our thoughts and actions.[42] People's intentions, including our own, typically are hidden from our view. Nonetheless, we can learn to notice them. If we don't notice them, then they will continue to influence our thoughts, feelings, and actions, and we will keep practicing them over and over in different situations. They will be overlearned and become a habit, one that will generalize to other, somewhat similar, situations. This is why you can start to notice people who have to have control, or have to be the victim, etc. They have practised these intentions to the point that these become habitual.

Once we learn to pay attention to our intentions, however, we begin to regain some control over them, rather than having them continue to control us. We can set intentions. We can cultivate certain goals and allow our intentions to perfume our thoughts, words, and deeds. This is why, for example, Buddhist practice puts so much emphasis on meditation techniques like compassion and loving-kindness—it is a practice designed to undermine our usual selfish intentions and instead begin to make caring intentions more habitual.

Step 2: Planning

Once we have a motivation to do or refuse to do something, we often reinforce that intention by planning. The intention is usually not sufficient, unless the action and the goal are trivial.

Let's return to Diane's story. After the birth of their daughter, Emma, David's attacks on Diane's schooling became more intense.

'I felt boxed in. David only wanted me to take classes that were directly related to the goal of my degree. Taking classes began to feel like a chore. I had no freedom to choose which classes to take. And even then, he kept complaining, even though I was only taking the classes he had approved.'

'I couldn't understand what I was doing wrong. I was trying to do something that could help our finances, that would open more interesting jobs for me. A previous person at my work had gone to work at a software development company that made the software my company used. That seemed really fun. I was good at programming, but I wanted a piece of paper that said, "Look, I'm competent."'

'Why did you need that?' I asked.

'Partly because it was a requirement for some jobs, but really because I felt I needed to prove I'm good enough.'

'So, after you finished a class, what would happen?'

'He would ask, "Aren't you finished yet?" He hadn't gone to college, and so he didn't really understand it's not about this class or that one, but about how all of them fit together by the end. I felt like I had to be sneaky to take classes, but there wasn't any way to be sneaky about it. Each new semester, I had to carefully look at the class schedules, check to see if he was working days or nights in his job, look at my work schedule for the next months, and check that we could have childcare regularly. There were lots of classes I couldn't take, just because one of these things didn't work out. Everything had to line up just right to even make taking one class possible.'

Diane had the intention to grow, to learn, and to set herself up for better possibilities that could be of benefit to herself and her family. This is why she went back to school. But simply having an intention is not enough. Instead, if we want 'good' outcomes of our intentions and to avoid 'bad' outcomes, some thought about how best to proceed can be useful. Diane had to plan carefully which classes were possible for her to take without it being a burden on the family.

Planning may be simple and quick, or it may be complicated and detailed. I, like many people, worry about potentially difficult conversations. My response to the anxiety is often to spend an inordinate amount of time rehearsing what I'm going to say, how I'll say it, how I'll react when they say something, and so on. Of course, the conversations never go as I planned them, but that doesn't mean I'm not still creating karma from all of my planning and rehearsing particular things I'd like to say.

From a learning psychology perspective, planning and rumination are types of cognitive learning, where we rehearse and self-reinforce ideas, motivations, and behaviours. Practicing these thoughts makes the odds of behaving in certain ways more likely and the odds of behaving in other ways less likely. This is another fair way to consider our internal karma at any given time—not all ways of acting are equally available to us in a given situation because we've planned and mentally practised some over others. More planning reinforces intentions and deepens the karma of an action when taken.

Step 3: Action

Once we've established an intention and planned a way to achieve our goal, we may take an action. Actions in Buddhist thought include mental actions, speech, and bodily actions, and each can produce effects. These effects can be internal, such as learning something better. When we rehearse a thought, the thought becomes more accessible in the future. As Diane took classes, she learned new ideas, which changed the way she thought. She began to grow in new ways and to care about new things. She began to see herself differently, as more competent. The effects can also be external, as the ripples flow outward from the action. As Diane grew and her interests broadened, David felt threatened and began to punish her for taking classes. As he punished her, it changed her feelings both about taking classes and about him. Actions beget reactions which beget actions and so on, as the ripples intersect.

I have a colleague that is difficult for me to deal with—I'll call him Steve. Steve is loud and opinionated, believes everything he thinks, which is a problem because he often thinks very unkind things about everyone else's motivations. In the past, Steve used to brag openly about how he would engage in unethical research practices and get away with them. I'm guessing that he probably got reprimanded at some point, because he's not as open about it anymore. Instead, he now regularly suggests that others are doing many of the same types of unethical and inappropriate things he used to do, with no evidence whatsoever. Once when he saw something of mine that he didn't understand, rather than coming to me to ask me about it, he complained to my supervisors and caused quite a fuss, spreading rumours that I was doing illegal things. After the full and thorough investigation, it became clear I had followed all the procedures correctly. Nonetheless, the rumour still persisted and caused me more trouble, such as not getting a promotion at the time I should have. You can see some of the ripples of karma here.

As you might imagine, I no longer have good feelings about Steve. I have witnessed him harming others many times, and have felt some of that harm myself. When I need to go into a meeting with him, I feel some distaste. Often the thought will arise, 'I just don't want to do this. He's going to say something mean and offensive.' Having had that thought as I walk into the room, what will happen?

I will likely be on high alert for him to say something annoying, and then I'll be much quicker to get angry because I've been on high alert. Psychologists call this 'priming,' where certain neural pathways get warmed up and ready to go. Not only are they faster to jump to conclusions, they will do it on much weaker evidence. I used to be annoyed only when Steve said something unkind or unfair. Now I get annoyed almost every time he opens his mouth, even if I previously would have agreed with what he is saying.

What if I walked into the room and instead of thinking about how Steve will likely say something offensive, I thought, 'Whatever happens, I can work with it.' How might that change me in the meeting? How might it change the whole flavour and outcome of the meeting? It's often much harder to see the karmic effect a thought has, especially because we are the only ones who know our thoughts. It's easy to fool ourselves into believing that our thoughts don't matter much or don't have much effect outside of our heads. Nothing could be farther from the truth.

Every time you have a thought, it is one more practice session, burning it deeper into your brain, making access to it easier, faster, and more automatic. This is why, for example, you can practice a golf or tennis swing in your head and it actually improves your real-world golf or tennis swing (assuming you practice the form correctly in your head). If you regularly think sarcastic and snarky thoughts about the people around you, even if you don't say them out loud, you become a nastier person. If you regularly think caring thoughts, even if you don't act on them, you will become more caring. This is why thoughts, words, and external actions all matter—all these can create karmic ripples for yourself and others.

> 'Even a thought which is unaccompanied by outward action, even so much as the moving of a muscle, is considered to produce specific kammic effect. Actual murder no doubt has greater effect than the mere thought of murder unaccompanied by any [bodily] action; yet, from the Buddhist point of view, even the latter is wrong.'[43]

Once we've taken some action, no matter the form, are we fated to suffer the consequences? Not necessarily. We can influence the reactions even after taking an action, depending on the attitude that we take toward the action.

Step 4: Non-remorse.

Imagine an alternative way in which things might have played out for David and Diane. David feels like Diane's going back to school is a threat. He feels like he's losing something, or perhaps he feels stupid in comparison. He feels taken advantage of, because he has to stay at home and take care of Emma while Diane is in class. In response, he has an intention to reduce this negative feeling, to regain control or balance. He rehearses a couple of choice things to say when Diane gets home from class as he fumes silently, watching Emma play with her Littlest Pet Shop animals.

He hears the car pull up into their garage. He stays seated on the couch in front of the television. He hears her come into the house, put down her purse and books. He gets tense, readying himself for the confrontation. She goes into the bathroom. Thwarted, he stews some more, getting angrier and thinking of more things to say. The door opens and he hears her come looking for them. She walks into the room and immediately knows something is wrong, despite Emma yelling 'Mommy's home!' and running to her.

Instead of looking at Diane and asking how her day was, David continues to look at the television. After a few moments of talking to Emma, Diane puts her down with her toys and goes to sit on the couch next to David. She places her hand on his arm, and he pulls away. She asks, 'How are you?'

He sits silently for a few minutes, as Diane sits back on the couch waiting for the inevitable. Finally he says, 'You just want to stay away from me and Emma, don't you?' He sees that his arrow has hit the target. Diane, who had entered the room bursting with vibrancy, seems to totally deflate.

You and I know that she has been injured by his intentionally harmful and planned actions and words. He knew too. If he felt a moment of regret upon seeing Diane's pained expression, we don't know about it. This is the fourth aspect of planting a karmic seed—non-remorse. What if he had recognized the damage he had done and then immediately apologized? The amount of damage would have been lessened, and in fact, it could have strengthened their relationship because it could have given them the opportunity to talk about their feelings. What if he went to bed feeling totally justified, but woke up realizing he had gone too far. He still wasn't willing to apologize, but did feel badly about being quite so harsh. This would lessen the odds that he would be so mean the next time, which still would likely help their relationship. What if he not only went to bed feeling justified, but continued to think of himself as the victim here and that he should have said even more of the choice things he had dreamed up? The odds that he'll do it again go up. The odds that it will cause a really huge ripple go up.

After taking an action, there is an opportunity to reflect upon it. If you did something harmful and feel remorse, this lessens the karmic force behind the action. In contrast, if you don't feel remorse, or worse, you rejoice for having caused harm, then the karmic force is increased. Thus, we can lessen the impact of our harmful actions by feeling remorse, and we can also increase the impact of our beneficial actions by rejoicing in them. Indeed, it is said that:

> 'When all four of these factors [intention, planning, action, and non-remorse] are present, the karma committed is very strong. When these factors are not all present, then it is not a complete karmic act. For example, if someone accidentally ran over a snake with a car there was no intention, no plan, and one possibly had remorse. Therefore, it is not a complete karmic act.'[44]

Tibetan teacher Traleg Kyabgon notes that two people can take the same action and yet have different karmic results. This is due in part to potentially different intentions, different characters of people, different conditions, and also different mitigating thoughts. He notes:

> The role of mitigating circumstances is similar to that of intention. The Buddha allowed for the relevant mitigating circumstances that might accompany the performance of a particular action. An individual who acts in a certain way would not necessarily experience the 'usual' consequences of that particular action, depending on the mitigating circumstances. For example, if we did a good deed and felt some misgivings or regret about it, then the merit attached to the good deed would be diminished. Conversely, if we performed a terrible— or even evil—deed, but felt regret after the fact, then the profoundly negative karmic consequences that might accrue would be diminished. Therefore, one person's acting in a particular manner does not mean that he or she will face the same consequences, or degree of consequences, as another person committing that same act. The Buddha actually said that we should not regret a good deed and we should regret an evil deed. In the former case, for instance, if we had generously given away something, only later to think, 'Oh, gee, what did I do?' then the potential merit that we would have accrued (had we not regretted it) ends up being diminished.[45]

Why is this? In learning theory terminology, if we regret our generous action, we are self-punishing, which makes the likelihood of engaging in a similar generous action less in the future. That's karma. If we rejoice in the bad action, we are self-reinforcing, making the likelihood greater in the future to do a similar bad thing. The consequences can therefore also be enhanced or mitigated by our reflection on our actions. We also see parallels in U.S. law for this. Once someone is convicted of a crime, the extent of punishment often hinges on how much remorse the perpetrator has shown. In Buddhist terms, the thought or feeling of remorse is one more action, and it can be used to reset future intentions.

Putting it All Together

This teaching demonstrates how karma is not fatalism. The Buddha denied that any given action always resulted in a specific effect. There are always multiple causes and conditions at play within the complex context of the action, relationship, history, etc. The Buddha's teaching demonstrates how and where we can have agency. We may not be able to undo something harmful we have done, but we can still feel remorse for it. This is considered a positive emotion in Buddhist psychology, because it recognizes the opportunity for change. We don't simply feel guilty, or punish ourselves. Instead, we recognize that we can change our behavior in the future, abstaining from causing more harm.

There is one more aspect of the law of causation which needs to be set forth and that is the relation between an effect and one's acceptance of it. We sometimes have a tendency to think that effects are irreversible since they result from primary and secondary causes. Nevertheless, depending upon our attitude, a bad effect may be turned to a good end. Suppose one is sentenced to jail. This is an effect of a previous action. How one chooses to accept the situation, however, is up to him. He may have a change of heart and become law-abiding or, as an old offender, tell himself to be more careful and not get caught the next time. On the other hand, he may make his jail his spiritual training centre by practicing zazen and reading good books. Obviously his attitude toward his confinement will greatly alter its effect upon him.

Fatalism, then, is a misconception of the Buddhist law of causation. Nothing is fixed ... Man and his environment are not separate and apart. One's situation is not ordered by either gods or devils but is a natural consequence of one's own actions. We express ourselves by thought, speech, and action even though we are unaware of the meaning of good and bad. These actions echo within us and influence our personality. When our attitudes change, our circumstances likewise change ..."[46]

Putting all of this together, in my view, the central message of Buddhism is that everything matters. Every thought, word, deed—every intention, rumination, reaction, and plan, they all have consequences. Therefore, we should pay attention in the moment, and we should pay attention to our intentions. The past karma has ripened into this moment. The future doesn't exist yet. We actually have total freedom in this moment, but we rarely recognize or exercise it. We will discuss this more in the chapters on free will.

CHAPTER 7: Karma in Relationships and Culture

Individual Karma

Up to this point, we have been examining karma primarily from our individual point of view. This chapter will broaden the view to see other aspects. Nonetheless, Karma is traditionally taught with reference to individuals, individual actions and their specific reactions. Our actions result in consequences that we will experience. This personal aspect is beneficial for helping us to recognize our personal responsibility in each moment, as well as to provide us with a guide for ethically-grounded behaviour. The Buddha stated that all people, lay or ordained, men and women, should regularly contemplate:

> 'I am the owner of my actions [karma], heir to my actions, born of my actions, related through my actions, and have my actions as my arbitrator. Whatever I do, for good or for evil, to that will I fall heir.' ... There are beings who conduct themselves in a bad way in body ... in speech ... and in mind. But when they often reflect on that fact, that bad conduct in body, speech, and mind will either be entirely abandoned or grow weaker ...
>
> A disciple of the noble ones considers this: 'I am not the only one who is owner of my actions, heir to my actions, born of my actions, related through my actions, and have my actions

as my arbitrator; whatever I do, for good or for evil, to that will I fall heir. To the extent that there are beings—past and future, passing away and re-arising—all beings are the owner of their actions, heir to their actions, born of their actions, related through their actions, and have their actions as their arbitrator. Whatever they do, for good or for evil, to that will they fall heir.' When he/she often reflects on this, the [factors of the] path take birth. He/She sticks with that path, develops it, cultivates it. As he/she sticks with that path, develops it, and cultivates it, the fetters are abandoned, the obsessions destroyed.[47]

This emphasis on taking personal responsibility for our actions and their consequences has sometimes had the unintended consequence of making people feel like they are responsible for everything that happens to them. This could only be true if you were the only person in the world. Because everyone else around you is acting, and actions affect others beyond the actor, we are also the inheritors of other people's karma, especially if we're in relationship with them.

If we only consider individual karma, it is easy to draw wrong and, indeed, harmful conclusions. Returning to Diane's story, for example, she chose to take college classes. This resulted in her husband's anger and repeated unkind reactions. Looking at it from the traditional simplistic individual view, 'Whatever people do, for good or for evil, to that will they fall heir,' we might be tempted to conclude that there was something wrong with her taking classes. Diane took classes and it seems to have injured David. Classically, this is how we test to see if our actions are skilful and wholesome—by seeing what fruit they bear. If people are harmed, then our action was likely unskilful. If they are benefitted, then it was skilful. But this is just a rule of thumb. It is a simple test that works much of the time, but it probably starts to break down when the actions are complex (such as going to college—it's not one action) and when we're in complex relationships with people (such as partners, parents, and children).

Diane

I sat down with Diane again another afternoon at a neighbourhood coffee shop. The speckled sunlight came in through the large bay windows, dappling several cozy corners with overstuffed chairs. She ordered a latte and I ordered an oolong tea. As I sank into the cool squeaky leather, I asked a question that had been perplexing me, 'Why didn't David see how going back to school, learning about computer programming, and getting a better job would be good for the whole family?'

'I don't know.' She paused, and thought for a moment. 'I guess he saw himself as the rule maker and the enforcer. If Emma did something he didn't like, such as crying or not sleeping, he would either tell me to make her stop, or he would yell at her so much that she would be terrified, shaking and trembling. Then I would have to hold her to try to calm her down. He didn't take care of Emma. That was my job. I had to give her baths, dress her, feed her. He was only interested in Emma when she was noisy. Then he'd tell her to shut up or tell me to tell her to shut up.

'By the time Emma was three, I had been reduced to only having a couple of basic functions. I was responsible for cooking, cleaning, and having sex. He couldn't just rub my shoulder without it meaning what I was supposed to do next. He wouldn't ever touch me unless it was an implicit command.

'We didn't talk about much, and half the time he would insult me for being smart.'

I started at this. 'How?'

'Well, if he was writing an email or something and I tried to correct his spelling, he would call me 'brainiac' or 'encyclopaedia'.'

'It sounds like he felt threatened by your intelligence?'

Diane shrugged. She took a sip of her latte. 'It wasn't just at home where he would check out of our relationship. He stopped wanting to go to places with me. One year I went to four weddings alone, including *his* cousin's wedding! I wanted to do things together, but he didn't want to engage with me. I had to make excuses for why he wasn't there.

He would say, 'Tell them I'm sick.' So I'd leave the house, and he'd be out mowing the lawn.'

'How did you handle it?'

'My meditation practice helped me. Every night I would meditate, sitting on the floor at the end of my bed. I would visualize letting go of all of the difficult stuff, the things not working ... it would be like breathing out brown chunky stuff, and breathing in clean and clear.'

'Was that enough?'

'For a while. But as things got worse, I got depressed. He wouldn't engage with me. He wouldn't spend time with me. I felt like there was a terrible weight on me. I would be bawling on the bathroom floor, not able to get up.'

'He noticed I was depressed and yelled at me for that, too.'

'Did you ask him to go to counselling with you?'

'Yes, but he said, "No—you're the one who's depressed. You go fix yourself and stop being so depressed."'

Diane put her cup on the table and looked away. Her hand trembled slightly as she let go of the cup. 'So I went to a therapist, but it didn't really help. The more I talked about what was bothering me, the angrier I got. I didn't want to be angry. So I quit going after a while.'

'But you were right to be angry. He was being cruel to you.' Now I was angry.

Diane sighed. 'I realized that being angry wasn't going to help things in that moment.

Meeting his anger with my anger hadn't changed anything. Maybe it was time to try a new approach.'

'What did you do?'

'Okay, first you have to realize that we had gotten to this place a little at a time, over the course of several years. He was stuck in his pattern of being pleasant to me when he was happy with me and refusing to talk to me when he disapproved of anything I was doing. I'm not an opinionated person, and for the first seven or so years of our marriage, I just went along with what he wanted. I don't really recall ever having any disagreements with him. But as I started having things that I cared about, things that were different from what he cared about, he didn't know how to handle that. As I took more classes, I wanted the growth more. But because we had never set up a good way of communicating about our difficulties, once we had different opinions or goals, we did things reflexively and badly.'

'We felt entirely stuck in this pattern,' she continued. 'No one thing had started it, and there wasn't a clear singular thing to improve it. Even though neither of us was happy about it, we felt kind of powerless. It's like it had a momentum of its own.'

This is a critical insight. Karma is not simply your individual habits, patterns, actions, and consequences. Relationships have habits, patterns, actions and consequences also. Relationships do have a momentum that is in addition to the karmic momentum of the individuals involved, because the relationship doesn't exist just within either of the individuals. Each action causes ripples that can trigger reactions that cause their own ripples, and these can compound to become giant waves. Diane's wanting to learn new things scared David. He reacted in a way that hurt Diane. She reacted by becoming depressed. He reacted by withdrawing more.

I looked out the window. The afternoon sunlight was turning more golden, in contrast to the mood of our conversation. Still, I knew a breakthrough was coming, and I wanted to know how it happened. 'What did you do to try to get unstuck?' I asked.

'Lots of things, most of which seem really silly now.' She swirled the last of latte around in the cup with a little grimace of embarrassment. 'I felt like I wasn't being noticed, like I was part of the wallpaper. I noticed that most of my clothes were very earth-toned ... black, brown, beige. So I bought a red jacket.' She paused, remembering. 'And a couple other things in bright colours that I usually wouldn't wear. I hoped it would make me visible.'

'Ha! I love it!' I exclaimed. 'How did he react?'

'Like I'd gotten a new haircut.' She looked at me meaningfully, then added, 'Didn't notice at all.'

'I tried other things. I once read an article about how to spice up your love life. It said you should buy your husband a tie, and when he comes home, you should be sitting there wearing the tie and nothing else. So I did that.' She finished her drink and put it down. 'He walked through the door and I said something like "Welcome home!" He looked at me puzzled, paused for a moment, then walked into the kitchen, got a snack, and went in to watch TV, leaving me sitting there naked with this stupid tie on.'

Relational Karma

Chögyam Trungpa, when asked, 'Can changing one's own karma affect the people around you? Would it change theirs?' answered by saying, 'Well, if you are around them, obviously. If you're freaking out, the others also might slightly freak out. It's very simple. There's nothing magical about karma.'[48]

As Diane recognized, understanding karma is about understanding why we are in the situation we're in, what the relationship is at that moment, why we're feeling the way we are, and then being clear about what our function is—what actions we can take given the constraints of the situation. We need to realize that our actions influence others, just as their actions influence us.

Relationships have a karma of their own, in addition to our individual karma. Relationships can get into patterns, run on habit energy, predispose us to see only some things and not others, and perpetuate cycles that can be either healthy or unhealthy. Past decisions and actions condition the present, so that only some types of opportunities appear available to us in the present moment. We get into the same arguments over and over, despite knowing the outcome will be the same again.

Relational karma does not, however, need the people to know each other to still be able to affect each other. Consider a drunk driver who runs a red light and injures you. Your injury is not simply your personal karma. You became injured primarily because of the *other person's* karma. They took actions of drinking and driving and making poor decisions—you didn't. They were heedless and ran the red light—you didn't. Nonetheless, your karma is changed by theirs. You may have to deal with the effects of the injury for years. Karma, therefore, is not only individual. You are not only the inheritor of your own karma, but also that of others.

To oversimplify, if we think of ourselves as billiard balls, we are moving in a particular trajectory because of our prior actions. Yet, another ball can hit us and change our trajectory. We inherit some of the karmic momentum of other people due to their actions, not our actions. This is still overly simplistic, because the pool table isn't perfectly flat and non-moving, and there are hundreds of balls in constant jostling motion all around us. In fact, it is surprising to me that we could ever have believed that karma is primarily an individual issue. One of the hallmarks of Buddhist insight and philosophy is that everything is interconnected and interdependent. If that is so, then any action I take can almost never affect only me—it must have consequences that ripple outward and influence many other beings. Conversely, others' actions must constantly be influencing me, although I will probably not be aware of it.

Imagine that you sign up for a project at a university. You are escorted by an experimenter to a small room in a building you don't know well. You are given a survey packet to complete, and the experimenter leaves the room and shuts the door. You are seated at a table, and although there are other chairs around the table, you are alone in the room. You can just hear the slight buzz of the fluorescent lights overhead. You adjust your seat, and begin filling out the survey packet with your Number 2 pencil. After a while, you notice the smell of smoke. You sit up and look around. Behind you up near the top of the wall is an air vent, and smoke is beginning to pour through it. You don't know the layout of this building, but that clearly doesn't seem like a good thing. You listen for a fire alarm, but hear nothing out of the ordinary. You look again. The smoke seems thicker now. It's unclear whether this is a serious problem or not—the smoke might signify that there is a fire starting somewhere in the building. What do you do?

If you're like most people, you get up, open the door and tell the experimenter about the smoke. When people were in the situation described above, 75 per cent of them got up and reported the smoke.[49] What would happen if we changed it so that there were two more people in the room with you? Imagine that the three of you are now escorted to the room and given your survey packets. You don't know the other two people, but they seem fine. You make a little small talk as you take your seats, but then each of you begin to focus on completing the surveys. Once again, smoke begins to come in the vent. You notice it, and you can see that the other two people have noticed it too. What do you do?

Based on the earlier study, we know that the odds are 75 per cent that any individual will report the smoke. Logically, the rate of reporting the smoke should go up if we add two more people in the room, because the odds for each one individually is 75 per cent. With three people in the room, (trust me on the math), 98 per cent of three-person groups should contain at least one person who would report the smoke. This isn't what happens. Once you have noticed that the other people also saw the smoke, you probably will just continue to fill out your packet as the room fills with smoke. Only 38 per cent of three-person groups report the smoke. That's half as many as when people are alone, even though mathematically, almost every group should report it! It gets worse. If the other two people are research confederates who were instructed to ignore the smoke, the percentage dropped to only 10 per cent of the real participants reporting the smoke.

Whether people were alone or in groups also changed how quickly they responded. Over half (55 per cent) of the participants reported the smoke within two minutes when they were alone, whereas only 12 per cent of the participants in the three-person groups reported it in that time. By four minutes, 75 per cent of the lone participants had reported the smoke as opposed to only 12 per cent of the three-people group. Perhaps people are less observant in groups? No. When asked afterwards, everyone had indeed noticed the smoke.

When asked why they did not report the smoke, people claimed they had decided the smoke was not dangerous, although they had a wide range of interpretations, including some believing it to be a truth serum gas to get better answers on the survey! The most interesting thing, however, is that no one realized what they were influenced by. The participants claimed that they paid no attention to the reactions of other people in the room. The accurate reason people didn't report the smoke is because there were others in the room—responding dropped from 75 per cent to 38 per cent or 10 per cent just by putting two other people in the room. Everything else was exactly the same. Yet, they were completely unaware of how their interpretations and actions were influenced by the others' presence.

We are easily and highly influenced by others' actions, and this influence changes our actions and reactions. Again, we inherit not only our own karma, but that of others. This is important, because it helps to get us out from under the weight of blaming the victims. In my experience, too many people believe that karma means that they are responsible for every bad thing that has ever happened to them. If you were abused as a child, that is *not* your karma. That was the perpetrator's karma—due to the perpetrator's actions, the child was harmed. The child just happened to be in the wrong place at the wrong time, but is going to have to deal with the consequences of being abused for a long time. The child's trajectory is changed due to someone else's actions. The idea that you are responsible for everything that happens to you is wrong and damaging. The theory of karma demonstrates that you are responsible for how you handle yourself, not that you are responsible for how others act.

> Traleg Kyabgon puts it this way:
> Agents themselves are also continually interacting with other agents. Logically, then, we need not feel compelled to identify ourselves with a single thing, a core element to our psyche as it is really a matter of being in a constant state of flux. In this sense, karma could be said to operate as streams of networking karmic processes, where all kinds of living, breathing individuals are involved.'[50]

Although I am unaware of the Buddha himself discussing this interconnected relational karma, he certainly experienced it in his lifetime. We tend to believe that the Buddha had a blissful existence, just because he was a fully awakened being, but he had a tough life in many respects. For example, his own cousin, Devadatta, tried to kill him on three occasions, in one case by hurling a rock down a cliff at the Buddha. Although the rock missed him, it splintered upon impact and sent a shard into the Buddha's foot. At least two Pali sutras mention how he dealt with this:

Now at that time, his foot had been pierced by a stone sliver. Excruciating were the bodily feelings that developed within him—painful, fierce, sharp, wracking, repellent, disagreeable—but he endured them mindful, alert, & unperturbed. Having had his outer robe folded in four and laid out, he lay down on his right side in the lion's posture, with one foot placed on top of the other, mindful and alert ...

[A] 'devata exclaimed in the Blessed One's presence, 'What a lion is Gotama the contemplative! And like a lion, when bodily feelings have arisen—painful, fierce, sharp, wracking, repellent, disagreeable—he endures them mindful, alert, and unperturbed![51]

Why did Devadatta try to kill him on three occasions? If we take the simple view of karma, that actions beget reactions, then we would assume that the Buddha must have done something to Devadatta first to cause this as the appropriate reaction. The Buddha must have thrown a huge rock into the pond to get that strong a wave in response, right? Yet, it seems highly unlikely that an enlightened being like the Buddha acted in ways that were so harmful that the correct reaction would be murder. Instead, it's a fairly human story. Devadatta was jealous. He wanted to be the leader. The murder attempts were not the Buddha's actions; they were Devadatta's. Nonetheless, once injured, the Buddha had to deal with the pain of the injury. We are told that the pain was 'fierce, sharp, [and] wracking,' and the Buddha lay there feeling the unpleasant sensations, 'not awake with worry, nor afraid to sleep.'[52]

The argument that we can inherit the effects of other people's karma does not mean that we get to blame others and relinquish our own responsibilities. A somewhat harsh example is described in the Milindapañha:

A more problematic case is that of King Vessantara. Vessantara gave his wife and children to a Brahman, thereby causing the children great anguish. Milinda's question, then, is whether such an act of charity is not excessive. Can an act which makes others suffer in this way lead to happiness and a heavenly rebirth? Nāgasena holds that it can, for Vessantara's gift indicates that he has relinquished all desire for personal pleasures such as his family had brought to him ... Nonetheless, cannot Vessantara be accused of lack of consideration, or even of cruelty, so far as his treatment of the children is concerned? Nāgasena claims not ... He argues that the children's anguish arose only because of their inability to understand the action of their father. Had they realized that the Brahman was a field of merit worthy of such a gift, they would have been happy to have played a role in their father's act of charity. Thus, their suffering derived from their own ignorance, rather than from any misdeed of their father.[53]

Two aspects interest me in this odd example. First, we can be harmed by others' actions, even if they had beneficial intent. Second, once others take actions that influence us, how we react to it is our responsibility again. This approach to relational karma has two benefits:

(1) It doesn't blame the victim for everything that happens around and to them.
(2) It recognizes that they are still responsible for their own emotions, thoughts, and actions.

Moving from Relational to Collective Karma

The view of relational karma I am describing is not held universally in Buddhism. Soto Zen Roshi Taisen Deshimaru, for example, in his seminars on karma stated, '... a man only receives the effects of his own karma and not that of others. The power of karma has no influence on others.'[54] If, however, we are interconnected and dependent upon a multitude of interdependent causes and conditions, then I do not see how this can be accurate. Even he seems to not buy his argument entirely, because a little later, Roshi Deshimaru argues, 'In modern times, the criminal is more and more common. Criminal minds increase, laws increase, and all becomes more complicated. This is the karma of civilization.'[55] He appears to be arguing for a collective karma, which we all inherit and have to deal with.

I accept this argument. Continuing the logic of interdependence, all of our relationships are embedded within a broader network across the globe. Actions I take in my house can have effects on the other side of the planet. For example, even if you have a zero carbon footprint and are therefore not contributing to climate change at all, you will still have to deal with the effects of climate change. This is not an entirely new idea. In a debate from 1925 (cited by McDermott), Dr. Luang Suriaybongs wrote:

> Although man creates his own individual Karma, whatever he does will have its effect on his environment, too. Thus, he, at the same time, has common family-Karma, a racial, a national Karma, or a group-Karma. The good he does will not only benefit himself but all others who live with and around him, that is, all sentient beings. And vice-versa, evil will not be suffered by himself alone.[56]

Some Buddhist philosophies argue that the karmic seeds that are planted can be maintained over lifetimes. I know of no reputable scientific evidence of this. Nonetheless, we can inherit karmic momentum whose ripples affect our entire lives. For example, if I knew how you acted with your mother at twelve months of age, I could predict what your adult romantic relationships are like with pretty good accuracy.[57]

You might have heard of the scientific protocol known as the 'Strange Situation'. It is typically conducted with 12-month-old babies and their mothers.[58] The basic idea is that you bring a baby into a room with several toys and you watch how they act. Do they feel comfortable exploring? What happens when a stranger enters the room and tries to interact with the baby? The mother leaves the baby alone with the stranger. How does the baby react? What if the baby is left totally alone? What does the baby do when the mother returns? It turns out that there are very specific patterns of reactions by infants to this situation.

The first pattern is where the baby is generally content to explore when the mother is present, cries when the mother leaves, is not particularly comforted by the stranger, and becomes happy when the mother returns, and can go back to exploring. This pattern is called demonstrating 'secure attachment'. The infant can use the mother as a base of exploration and feels safe when the mother is present. This pattern of infant behaviour is predicted by the mother's behaviours over the past year. Secure attachment is predicted by sensitive and responsive parenting. When the baby cries, the mother immediately and consistently tries to figure out what is needed and give it to the baby. Thus, the baby learns that it can trust the mother to be there when needed.

The second pattern is very different. These babies do not cry when the mother leaves the room and do not seem particularly happy when the mother returns. They act as if they aren't comfortable expressing their emotions very openly. This pattern is called 'avoidant attachment', and it is predicted by mothers who are rejecting, or at the extreme, abusive toward their babies. We can imagine when the baby cries, the mother ignores the baby, gives it something it doesn't need, or perhaps even hits or punishes the baby for crying. The infant learns, therefore, that it does not help to cry because it won't get what it needs.

The third main pattern is where babies cry when the mother leaves, but they don't stop crying when she returns. They act as if they can't get enough love and comfort to be able to settle down. This pattern has been called several things, including 'anxious attachment'. This pattern is predicted by inconsistent parenting. Sometimes the parents are sensitive and responsive, and sometimes they are insensitive, intrusive, or rejecting. Imagine the pattern in these infants' houses, sometimes when babies cry they get what they need, and sometimes they don't. They can't predict what will happen this time. It's as if when they're getting what they need, they become extra needy and clingy to try to get as much as they can this time because they might not get it next time.

Because semantic word- or story-based memory has not yet begun (which is why most people's earliest memories begin at about age three), you will not have any memories of how you mother interacted with you during your first year. Nonetheless, the ripples from these early experiences continue into adulthood. If you were securely attached as an infant, you tend to be open, comfortable with closeness, trusting, and able to express and accept love in your adult romantic relationships.

If, however, you were avoidant attached as an infant, you continue these patterns into your adult romantic relationships, being more likely to be distant, cool, untrusting, and not willing to show your emotions easily to your partner. If you were anxious attached as a 12-month-old, you are likely to be clingy, jealous, and dependent in your adult romantic relationships. Have you dated each of these three types? Do you see which one you are most like? Well then, I guess we can say it really *is* your mother's fault!

That said, now that you are aware of it, only you can do anything about it. Once we become aware of our karma, even karma that was imparted to us by others, we gain the opportunity to change it. If we simply blame our past for where we are now, we continue to stay stuck in our patterns. You are the only person who can work with your karma.[59]

How, though? Especially when we feel stuck, it can be overwhelming to try to figure out where to put our limited energy. To understand where to be most effective, we need to understand what free will is and what it isn't.

CHAPTER 8: Free Will Isn't as Free as We Believe

Please complete the following little puzzle quickly. Try to go with your first ideas rather than over-thinking it.

Think of a number between 1 and 10.   Write it here: _____
Multiply it by 9.   × 9 = _____
Add the two digits together (e.g., 18 would be 1 + 8).   = _____
Subtract 5 from your answer.   − 5 = _____
Find the letter of the alphabet that is associated with
that number. (A is 1, B is 2, C is 3, etc.)   Letter is: _____

Think of a country beginning with that letter.
                                        Country is: _____
Take the last letter of that country's name, and
think of an animal that begins with that letter
(e.g., England ends with D, so that might be 'dog').
                                        Animal is: _____
Take the last letter of the animal's name, and think
of a colour that starts with that letter.
                                        Colour is: _____

Please complete this before turning the page.

I'm sorry, but you will never find an orange kangaroo in Denmark (nor an indigo kiwi). About nine out of ten people in America will provide this answer. Given that everyone has free will to begin with any number and to choose any country, animal, and colour, how can I predict what most people will say? Because although we often think that free will is doing or saying whatever we want, that isn't really what it is.

Despite having apparent total freedom of choice about what to pick, most people will pick the same thing. Why? First, our situation often includes constraints of which we are not aware—this is fixed karma. In this example, no matter what number you begin with, you will end up with the number 4 (e.g., $2 \times 9 = 18$, $1 + 8 - 5 = 4$). In English, this yields the letter D. So I know everyone must start with the letter D.

The second and more interesting reason, however, is because our prior learning can control our futures—this is old karma or the karma of result. Although there are six countries that can be considered to start with the letter D in their English names, almost everyone will choose the same one because of our past conditioning and the availability heuristic—what comes to mind first is the thing we've had the most experience with; it's more available to conscious thought. In this case, Denmark is more likely to come to mind for most people than the Democratic Republic of the Congo. Yet, despite how predictable people generally are, we do not like to believe that we are influenced outside of our conscious awareness.

People in the United States, Hong Kong, Columbia, and India were asked whether they believed that everything that happens is completely caused by whatever happened before it or whether human decision making was exempt from prior causality. An overwhelming majority of people in all countries thought that human decision are separate from their conditions. Most people disagreed that our actions are caused by prior conditions.[60] We like to believe we're in control of at least part of our lives, and we especially believe we're in control of our actions. This is part of why we like thinking so much. Thinking about the future, the past, or what we are doing gives a real sense of having some control. Unfortunately, this is an illusion.

We are sometimes aware of being influenced by our past or the situation, despite our thoughts. For example, if I had a bad experience with a dog, I might fear other new dogs, despite never having any bad experiences with them specifically. Our feelings about things are regularly conditioned by our past experiences, such as was shown in the Little Albert experiment. This operates at a level where thinking doesn't really have much sway because of how the brain evolved. We can tell ourselves there is no reason to be scared of this new dog who looks so friendly, but simply thinking that does not remove our fear. When we pay attention, we can often recognize how we are carrying old feelings and thoughts into a new situation. That doesn't immediately solve the issue, but it gives us some control. We will discuss more about how to recognize and exercise this control in Chapter 10.

What is much harder to recognize is how easily our behaviours can be influenced by external forces without our conscious awareness. Humans are surprisingly easy to manipulate, if you know the tricks.

Psychologist John Bargh and his colleagues performed a very clever set of experiments that demonstrated how easily we can be influenced by experiences and yet remain unaware of how we were influenced.[61] Imagine that Jack and Jill participate in a study with various tasks. First an experimenter takes them down a hallway to individual testing rooms and gives them each a packet of thirty five-word scrambled sentences to unscramble (e.g., 'it instantly he hidden finds'). They are told that once they finish the language task, they are to find the experimenter, who will be in a different room, and will take them to the next part of the study. Jill opens her packet and begins. Fifteen of the thirty sentences she unscrambles are like 'they her bother see usually.' Fifteen of Jack's are like 'they her respect see usually.'

It takes Jill only about five minutes to unscramble all thirty sentences, and feeling pleased, she returns the papers in the envelope, and leaves the room. She doesn't immediately see anyone when she steps out into the hallway. As she turns the corner, however, she sees the experimenter standing in the doorway of another testing room. The experimenter has the door half open and is talking to another study participant who appears to be having some difficulty understanding something. Jill walks near and stands quietly, waiting for the experimenter. The experimenter doesn't acknowledge Jill because she is talking to the other participant. This goes on for some time and Jill gets impatient, wanting to move on to the next task. Jack's experience is the same. How long do they each wait until they interrupt the experimenter?

If you're like the typical person who got the same sentences Jill did, you wait for a little more than five minutes before interrupting. Does that sound like a lot? If you had gotten the words Jack did, however, you would have waited almost twice as long! Why?

Three versions of sentences were created: One in which fifteen of the thirty sentences primed *polite* ideas (e.g., honour, considerate, appreciate, courteously, unobtrusively), another where fifteen sentences primed *rude* ideas (e.g., disturb, intrude, annoyingly, bluntly, obnoxious), and one with all neutral sentences (e.g., exercising, flawlessly, normally). As you've already heard, the participants in the rude priming condition were much more likely to interrupt the experimenter in a subsequent task.

When asked whether the sentence unscrambling task had any effect on them and how long they waited, people said, 'Certainly not!' But that was not true.

The participants were entirely unaware of how the earlier task influenced them. The authors concluded that the results 'point to a direct effect on behaviour that is not mediated by conscious, perceptual, or judgmental processes'.

Now that you're aware of how the process works, consider what might happen if we changed the sentences to include words that are relevant to a stereotype of elderly people (e.g., old, lonely, bingo, wrinkle, etc.). After completing the language task, participants left the lab and walked down the hallway to the elevator, but they walked slowly to the elevator—like an old person—compared to a control group who got neutral words. Again, they were completely unaware that the words influenced how they walked.

A third study used photographs presented so fast that people didn't know they saw anything. This priming caused people to be more hostile. Are you generally hostile? Probably not. But if you had been in the study, having certain photos shown to you subliminally would still have affected you.

The point is that these studies provide proof how we can be manipulated by things in our environment. Both our physical and emotional behaviours can be easily influenced without our knowledge or conscious awareness.

So, are our actions and feelings happening from our free will? If we can be manipulated without knowing it, are we in control of our actions?

This power to manipulate is used all the time by advertisers and marketers. For example, a store once made a simple test. They put some good quality men's shirts on sale, and had a sign describing the sale on the same table as the shirts. They kept track of how many shirts were sold in a week. The next week they kept the sale going—same shirts, same price, same sign, same location in the store. They changed one thing—the table. They changed it from a stainless steel table to a wooden table. Sales increased 30 per cent.

Why?

The scientifically correct answer is that we don't know. There are several hypotheses. Perhaps the wood seemed warmer, and made customers more interested in touching the shirts. There is a whole science of touch in stores, and your relationship with products changes drastically once you touch them. Perhaps the wood reminded people of home, so people wanted to take the shirts home with them. Would you even notice the table if you were shopping? Of course not! You're looking at the shirts, not the table.

Marketers don't know why this works. They don't care. It works! People can be influenced to change their behaviours without their knowledge or consent, and they will never even believe that they didn't have total free will. They will say it was entirely their decision, but it wasn't entirely.

If we are unaware that we're being influenced, then by definition, we are unaware of any external influence and we will maintain the illusion that we are in total control of our actions. In contrast, sometimes we think that we aren't in control, when we actually may be. For example, when under hypnosis, we may be aware that we are taking actions, but we do not see it as our choice. Similarly, when playing with a Ouija board, we may feel like the motions we are making with our hands are somehow not in our control.

The good news is that we already have some ability to perceive what is happening, and this perception can be sharpened.

The classic study in psychology on acting but believing that our actions are not our choice is known as the Milgram experiment on obedience.[62] Forty adult men between twenty and fifty participated in the original study. Upon arriving, they met a likeable forty-seven-year-old man who was introduced as another participant. They were apparently randomly assigned into the roles of teacher and learner, although the real participant was always in the role of teacher. They were told that the purpose of the study was to test the value of punishments on learning. Everyone was given a sample 45-volt shock on the wrist to see how it worked. Even 45 volts is somewhat painful. The 'learner,' however, was strapped to a chair in a different room and hooked up to a shock generator that the 'teacher' controlled:

> Each switch is clearly labelled with a voltage designation that ranges from 15 to 450 volts. There is a 15 volt increment from one switch to the next, going from left to right. In addition, the following verbal designations are clearly indicated for groups of four switches going from left to right: Slight Shock, Moderate Shock, Strong Shock, Very Strong Shock, Intense Shock, Extreme Intensity Shock, Danger: Severe Shock. (Two switches after this last designation are simply marked XXX.) Upon depressing a switch: a pilot light corresponding to each switch is illuminated in bright red; an electric buzzing is heard; an electric blue light, labelled 'voltage energizer,' flashes; the dial on the voltage meter swings to the right; various relay clicks are sounded.

The teacher is told to give the learner pairs of words, and to give a shock when the learner makes an error. Critically, with each new error, the teacher is told by the experimenter to move one level higher on the shock generator. At high shock levels, the learner pounds on the wall and screams and then later falls silent, answering none of the teacher's questions (in reality, this was scripted – the learner never received any shocks but the teachers believed he did). The teacher is told to continue giving shocks and then moving to the next question, despite not receiving any answer. A majority (26 out of the 40) continued until they gave the maximum possible shocks. In follow-up studies, similar results were obtained even when the participant was told upon meeting that the learner had a heart condition. Although the participants were often visibly and verbally distressed, they just kept giving higher and higher shocks. Why would they do that? The accurate but upsetting answer is because there was a young man in a lab coat telling them that they should. Despite the fact that the experimenter really had no authority at all over them, the participants felt like they had to keep giving shocks and that it wasn't their choice. We sometimes know we are acting but still do not feel like it is our thoughts and will that caused it.

This power can become even stronger and more insidious when people are in groups. For example, in my college town, we have had several riots during party weekends. No one went out with the intention to riot—they went out to drink and dance and have a good time. But once people are in groups, it only takes two or three people to do something destructive and then the whole crowd can easily begin burning and smashing things. When asked why they participated, people feel like they really don't know why they did it even though they are quite aware that they were in control of their actions.

In Diane's story, she gave up her dream of going to college. This was her choice, but it also wasn't. She was being manipulated and pressured, sometimes directly and sometimes indirectly. She gave up her power, her agency. Did she need to? I can't answer that for her. I can, however, say that when we realize how easily we are manipulated and we become more aware of noticing those pressures, we gain the ability to resist them. Our free will is only free when we're clear and aware of how it may be being influenced by our past conditioning and the present situation.

CHAPTER 9: Our Thoughts Don't Necessarily Cause Our Actions

In the last chapter, we noticed that there are many things that influence and manipulate us that we are typically not aware of. These may be intentional, such as advertisements implanting small ideas and feelings in your head that later will create a willingness to try a product. When you decide to try that new shampoo, you will believe it is entirely your free will making the choice, but it isn't entirely. Many, if not most, of the aspects that influence us, however, are unintentional. These include internal aspects, such as neural, dispositional, biological, social, cognitive biases, and learned or conditioned causes that contribute to our actions (inner karma), as well as the situational and environmental aspects (outer karma). We therefore are influenced by a wide range of aspects in any given situation. Maybe this is why we seem to try so hard to plan and control things.

Diane told me, 'When I would leave work and drive to campus for my class, I couldn't just enjoy the drive or think about what I was learning. I was already worried about what David would say when I got home. I would plan a couple of different things I would say in response, and imagine how he'd react, and what I would say then. I'd rehearse how I would say these things, sometimes saying them out loud in my car just to hear how my voice sounded. All the way to school and then all the way back home, I'd plan and rehearse.' She smiled wryly.

'Of course, nothing ever went as planned.'

I expect this is familiar to most people. I certainly have done this a lot, especially if I'm going into what I expect might be a difficult situation. It never helps as much as I expect, and sometimes has actually made things worse. So why keep doing it?

There are, at least, two reasons. First, if rehearsing seems to help us manage the situation even just one out of ten times, then we have been intermittently reinforced for it. As you may recall, variable reinforcement is the best way to have a behaviour continue, even if it fails to work more times than it does. Second, and more relevant to our discussion here, it gives us a feeling of control, and that feeling is reinforcing. We never ask, however, *why* does it give us a feeling of control?

Modern science is beginning to answer this question. It turns out that our conscious awareness tricks us into believing that our thinking helps us to be in control.

Imagine standing by a pool table with two balls on it. A red ball runs into a black ball, and the black ball immediately begins moving. What will you assume? You will assume that the red ball *caused* the black ball to begin moving. This is such a natural assumption your brain makes that you may have never realized that you actually have no real evidence about what caused the black ball to move. Our eyes don't see kinetic energy and energy transfer directly. They don't see causality directly. They just see motion and we infer causality. It's possible there is a mechanism under the table that made the red ball appear to hit the black ball, and the black ball was actually pulled along by a magnet. The point is that we really don't know. We assume causality. We're usually right, by the way. That's why we don't even think to question the assumption.

We see tree leaves moving and we assume the wind is causing the movement, even though we never see the wind. Similarly, we see our minds move, and we then assume that our thoughts cause our actions.

The late Harvard Professor Daniel Wegner conducted many studies demonstrating that our thoughts give us a feeling of free will and control, especially under three specific circumstances: Priority, Consistency, and Exclusivity.[63]

Priority

One reason that we believe our thoughts give us control is because they often happen before something else. In the pool ball example above, the red ball hits the black, immediately after which the black ball begins moving. When something happens right before something else, our brains use that as a cue for assuming causality. Again, it's often right. If you call me an idiot and I immediately get angry, you can probably correctly assume my anger was a response to your statement. The point is, however, it's an assumption. All assumptions are wrong some of the time.

In one of my favourite studies ever, imagine this scenario. You arrive at the study and are paired with another person, who is called the 'hand helper.' You put on headphones and gloves, as does the hand helper. The hand helper stands immediately behind you and sticks her arms out under yours and puts them through the arms of a smock you are wearing. From your perspective, when you look down, you see hands coming out from about where your arms should be.[64]

You are told that you will hear a series of statements that might or might not relate to the actions of the hand helper. In your headphones, you hear, 'Wave hello with your left hand,' and then you see the hand helper's left hand (which is sticking out from under your armpit) wave. You hear 'Give the OK sign with both hands,' and you see both hands make this hand motion. After twenty-six of these messages and motions, you are given a survey asking you how much you had controlled the hand motions.

You *know* that they weren't your hands. Your hands were at your sides the whole time. You know that the hands you saw when you looked down were someone else's.

If you were in a condition where you didn't hear the words in your headphones, then you accurately state that you had no control over the arm motions you saw. But if you heard the words in your head right before you saw the action, you will report that you were somewhat in control!

This seems crazy. When participants heard the instructions, they were experiencing significantly more feeling of control, despite the fact that they all clearly knew that the arms weren't theirs! They weren't stupid. These were normal college students. But even knowing that they had absolutely no control, thinking of an action just before the action is performed made them feel like they had caused it.

This was replicated in additional studies, also showing that timing of the instruction mattered. Apparent causality was highest when the instruction was 3 seconds before the action, next highest when it was simultaneous, and lowest when it was heard 3 seconds after the action.[65] Thus, having a thought of something right before it happens makes us believe the thinking caused the action, even when it clearly did not.

This demonstrates the principal of priority—when we think something shortly before we do it, we believe that the thought *caused* the action, just the same as when we see one ball hit another, we believe the first ball caused the second to move. In both of these cases, we are making an assumption of something we don't actually see. We see one thing move and then another, but we do not see the causation directly— we infer it.

If you are not yet convinced, consider this thought experiment. If the five ball hits the eight ball, but the eight ball stays still for ten seconds and only then begins to move, would you still think the five ball caused it? If the eight ball began to move shortly before the five ball got to it, would you still think the five ball caused the eight to move? Our brains are set up to immediately assume causality under some circumstances, but not others. We rarely question why we perceive causality the way we do.

Consistency

Now, consider that the five ball hits the eight ball, and the eight ball begins rolling in the same direction that the five had been going. Again, we believe that the five caused the action in a way. We would not feel as strongly if the eight ball began rolling in a very different direction. If the five strikes the eight head on, but the eight begins rolling in a direction that is 90 degrees to the left of the direction the five had been going, we assume something else is going on. This is the principle of consistency. We infer causality when the result appears consistent with the cause. Does this happen with our thoughts too? Sometimes, our thoughts match what happens afterwards, and when thoughts are consistent with what happens, we experience it as mental causation.

Imagine that you have gone to a two-person study, but you arrive before your partner. You are told by the experimenter that this is a study on voodoo, based on a 1942 paper out of the Harvard Medical School. You read this short paper, which is an actual report that claims that illnesses and death can be caused by voodoo.[66] Your partner finally arrives, very late for the study. He is wearing a T-shirt with the slogan, 'Stupid people shouldn't breed,' appears not to really pay much attention to the instructions, is chewing gum with his mouth open, and sits there spinning his pen on the desk, while reading the voodoo paper. The experimenter gives you both a copy of the consent form to keep for your records. Your partner crumples it up and throws it in the garbage can. He misses. He shrugs and leaves the paper lying on the floor.

The experimenter tosses a coin, and you are given the role of 'witch doctor.' Your job is to stick pins into a voodoo doll representing your partner (the 'victim') while generating vivid thoughts about the victim. Your partner meanwhile fills out a survey about his current health. He circles 'No' to each of the twenty-six possible problems, and writes down 'Fine. No problems' at the bottom of the page. He writes his name on it, and this paper is affixed to a straw voodoo doll, which now represents him.

You are given five pins, and told to stick them in the head, heart, stomach, and the left and right sides, the 'weak parts' of the body. You have found your partner somewhat annoying, so you have no real problem doing this. The doll sits on the table between you and your partner, five pins sticking out of it.

Your partner is again given the physical symptom checklist, but this time he circles 'Yes' for a headache, and writes at the bottom, 'I have a bit of a headache now.' The experimenter looks at this, and asks him to verify that he now has a headache. Your partner looks uncomfortable, but confirms it. The experimenter asks your partner to step into another room so that they can ask some detailed questions about the physical symptoms. Your partner leaves, and the experimenter gives you some surveys to fill out.

There are several surveys, but two of the questions ask you, 'Did you feel like you caused the symptoms that the 'victim' reported, either directly or indirectly?' and 'Do you feel that your practice of voodoo affected the victim's symptoms?' You say that yes, it did seem to you like you caused the headache, at least somewhat.

Now consider a slightly different variation of the same study. Instead of being late and rude, your partner arrives on time and is attentive and polite. He still initially says he has no problems, but also gets a headache after you stick the pins into the doll. When asked whether you thought you caused the headache, you don't feel the headache was related to your actions much at all.

What makes this difference? Your thoughts. When your partner was rude, you had negative thoughts about him. When he was polite, you did not have any negative thoughts about him. Having negative thoughts just before he got a headache makes you think that you had some causal power over it, because the result is consistent with your thoughts.

That is, although the actions were the same every time—sticking pins in the voodoo doll—participants who had not generated negative thoughts were less likely to believe they had affected the victim. This demonstrates the principle of consistency—we believe our thoughts are more causal when they are in line with the alleged effects.

This also explains why people also believe in the stripped-down version of karma being a type of cosmic retribution. Your ex treated you badly and later has his heart broken. You feel that he got his comeuppance, that the universe was getting him back for being unkind to you. He got what he deserved, and you were part of the reason behind it. But if you were the one to treat your ex badly, and he has his heart broken again by his next relationship, you don't feel that the universe was in alignment. He didn't get what he deserved, and you don't feel that you were the cause of it. Karma is not a series of checks and balances, but when things line up the way we want, we feel like there is some causal power behind it.

For example, people do a lot of superstitious things to try to help situations that they have no control over. I am a lifelong fan of the American football team, Buffalo Bills. In the 1990s, when they were in four consecutive Superbowl championships, I did a lot of things to help them win. In the year that Doug Flutie was quarterback, my friend Thomas P. and I sat watching the game eating bowl after bowl of Flutie Flakes cereal, expecting that it would help him win. When more help was needed, we ate faster, shovelling spoon after spoon of the crunchy sweet flakes into our mouths. The Bills still lost. Had they won, however, we would have taken credit for the win.

Studies show that when people are watching a sport and the player they like scores a point, the people feel like they had some causal power over it.[67] If they were thinking about other things about the player when the player scored, they don't feel like they caused it the same way. When events happen in a way that is consistent with the way we feel, we again assume some causal power, even when it is logically clear that we had no causal agency over the event.

Exclusivity

As we have discussed, there are almost always myriad causes and conditions impinging on events at the same time. Yet, we can only know and perceive so much at one time. We are often unaware of most of the pressures that exist, so when we try to understand what caused something, we usually choose things that we can see. One more way our brains try to detect evidence of causation is by trying to notice how many things may have had an influence on a result. If we only see one obvious cause, with no competing alternatives, we assume the obvious.

Consider three pool balls all hitting the eight ball at once. We don't have strong feelings about any one of them being the cause of the eight-ball beginning to move. It gets even less clear if one end of the table is lifted … was it the balls or the tilt that caused the eight ball to move?

Similarly, we know about our thoughts, but we often don't know what else is influencing a situation or person. Therefore, we will believe our thoughts caused something when our thoughts are the only apparent plausible explanation for our actions.

The voodoo study above also demonstrates the exclusivity principle, as there didn't seem to be any other known reason as to why the victim would suddenly get a headache, other than the thoughts of ill intent while putting pins in the voodoo doll. It is difficult, however, to isolate each of these principles as they often co-occur (as in the voodoo study, which demonstrates to some extent temporal priority, consistency, and exclusivity).

In another clever study, people were hypnotized to perform an action. Would they feel like they caused the action? What if you also hypnotized them to not remember the command? After hypnotizing the people, they were given this command:

A little later, you will hear a noise like this [*a shuffling noise was played through the loudspeaker*]. When you hear this noise, you will cover your ears with both of your hands. You will cover your ears with both of your hands when you hear (*noise played*) but you will not remember my telling you anything about it … You will remember nothing until I say, 'Now you can remember everything.'[68]

After waking up from hypnosis, the people were put in a room with various toys and materials and were told to do whatever they wanted. They were also told that from time to time, a buzzer would sound and that they were to report three things:

(1) whatever they were doing at that moment,
(2) how intentional it felt, and
(3) the reason why they did it (which could be 'no reason').

The buzzer sounded seven times while they were doing various things, such as stretching or playing with a given toy. One of the times, the buzzer was sounded immediately after the noise was played and all the people covered their ears, despite the fact that the noise was not particularly annoying. Participants felt that most of their actions were highly intentional, but covering their ears was much less intentional than the other actions. That is, they knew why they were playing with a ball and felt they intended to do it, but they didn't know why they covered their ears, so they felt that it wasn't intentional.

This study included one additional trick. Half of the people were told by the experimenter over the intercom, 'I'm sorry, but I have to move some microphones around next door and it is going to cause a nasty feedback noise over the intercom.' Immediately after saying this, the 'cover ears' noise was played, followed by the buzzer. Everyone covered their ears as they had been hypnotized to do. These people, however, felt that they caused themselves to cover their ears.

As seen in Figure 6, giving people a reason for why they might cover their ears made their ear covering seem more intentional, despite the fact that it was not the real reason they covered their ears. They covered them because of the post-hypnotic suggestion, not because it was too loud a noise—in pilot testing with non-hypnotized people, no one covered their ears when hearing the noise, even after being given the same reason. Thus, if we can think of a reason why we might do something, it makes us feel more like we did it intentionally.

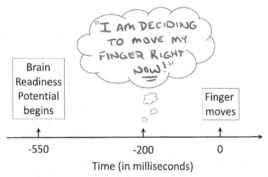

Figure 6: Average perceived intentionality for covering the ears with a fake reason, without the reason, and for all other voluntary comparison actions. All bars are significantly statistically different from each other.

Dr. Wheatley noted that:

Hypnotically suggested actions do not feel like other actions. Even though the action of covering one's ears is never normally an unintentional act, its intentionality was rated [much] lower than normal actions … The fact that the ear-covering felt so unintentional and yet looked so dramatically intentional, may suggest that the will is not simply observing the connection between one's thoughts and acts, but includes an internal experience to which observers lack access.[69]

This idea that our experience of free will is due to knowing our thoughts will be explored in the next chapter.

Thoughts and Actions

Who knows what you're thinking? Only you. As we've seen, when our thoughts come before an action and are consistent with the result, we feel like our thoughts caused the action. If there are competing reasons for a result, we feel less causal power. Nonetheless, we often still feel some, as in the case of the sports fan thinking wearing a special shirt 'helped' their team win. When we can't come up with other competing reasons, then if we have a thought, we again make the assumption that our thought caused the action. Recall the experiment where people were hypnotized to cover their ears; but if they were told there would be feedback, people felt that their ear-covering was intentional, even though it was still being controlled by the hypnotic suggestion. We know our thoughts, and if there is no known outside force, we think our thoughts caused our actions. This demonstrates the principal of exclusivity—we believe our thoughts are causal because we know our thoughts, but don't know other reasons something happened.

In all of the studies we discussed in this chapter—hand helper, voodoo, covering ears—notice that the actual author of the action was never the self, but that the self was felt to be the author. We believe that we are causal agents even when we aren't. Apparent authorship can be influenced by a variety of factors, including the timing of thinking and acting, the consistency with which our thoughts match actions in the world, the transparency of other possible interconnected causes, and the availability of a plausible 'reason' for actions. These studies do not say our thoughts have no effect—they certainly can, and sometimes do, have great effects. If we think something repeatedly, the odds go up that we'll do it later. Nonetheless, these studies demonstrate that our experience of thoughts causing actions is an illusion a great deal of the time.

CHAPTER 10: Free Will Isn't What We Think It Is

In the last chapter, we discussed how we mistakenly believe that our thoughts cause our actions. If our thoughts don't cause our actions, what does? Spoiler alert: we have free will, but it isn't what we usually experience and believe to be our free will. To understand this, we have to break down our experience of free will and look inside the brain a bit.

By hooking people up to a skull cap with electrodes, researchers can measure how and when the brain responds to various external and internal stimuli. When people are asked to do a simple voluntary motion, such as moving a finger, it turns out that you can see the brain getting ready to perform the action before the action is performed, this was called a 'readiness potential'.[70]

Neurologist Benjamin Libet wondered where conscious will is in relation to the readiness potential. Imagine that you are seated in a lab, and an EEG skullcap is placed on your head. These are like rubber swimming caps, with dozens of wires sticking off of it, connected to the EEG machine. The cap has electrodes that can pick up the brainwave patterns with great precision in timing.

An electrode is also placed on your finger, so it can measure whether you move it. You are asked to move your finger a little. As you do, the EEG machine records how your brain changes to start your finger moving and how it changes once you've completed the small movement.

There is a lot of scientific equipment in the room. Directly in front of you is an oscilloscope with a clock face on it, and a dot spinning very

Figure 7: The setup for the Libet experiment, where the timing of brain activity, the time of conscious decision, and the time of action can all be measured precisely

fast around the clock. You are asked to move your finger, and to notice the position of the dot when you make your conscious decision to move your finger (Figure 7).

You stare at the moving dot and decide 'Now!' to move your finger. When we examine what is happening in your brain, a fascinating pattern emerges.

Let's say you decided to move your finger when the dot was at the 12:00 position on the clock. It turns out that your 'decision' occurs about 200 milliseconds, or about $1/5^{th}$ of a second before the action.[71] This feels intuitively right—we make a decision to act and the action occurs shortly after the decision. Our thought happens just before the action. The thought caused the action, right?

Wrong.

We can see that your brain decided to move your finger about a half second *before* you became conscious of your decision. The readiness potential in your brain began between about 400 and 800 milliseconds *before* you became aware of your choice to act (Figure 8). If your brain 'decided' to act before you consciously knew it, who made the decision to move your finger? If you believe yourself to be consciously aware of your thoughts and actions, then someone else must have decided to act. The conscious thought or decision is the result of some other process, and is not the thing exercising free will.

Modern neuroscience seems to suggest that the *experience* of conscious will is an illusion. We believe that our consciously known thought is the author of the actions, but often that is not true. There is some unconscious process that does two things—it prepares the body for taking an action and it simultaneously prepares the mind for taking the action.

There is something in you that makes decisions, but it isn't your thoughts. Your thoughts are a result of it. Similarly, your actions are a result of it. The 'you' that decided probably doesn't need to think in linear concepts or words.

Maybe this is shocking to you, and maybe it feels right, now that you think about it. You have probably had the experience where you were deciding between two things. As you consider the pros and cons of each, it becomes clear that one of these things makes more logical sense. Your thought process makes it apparent that option A is the better one.

Figure 8: Timing of the brain's readiness potential. The action occurs at 0. Awareness of the choice to move occurs ~200 milliseconds before the action, but the brain has already been getting ready for several hundred milliseconds before that.

Still, you choose option B. Why? You don't really know, but you also know it feels right. Who made that decision, given that your thinking said you should choose A?

Wegner and Wheatley said it this way:

We can never be sure that our thoughts cause our actions, as there could always be unconscious causes that have produced them both. The impression that a thought has caused an action rests on a causal inference that is always open to question—yet this impression is the basis of the experience of will.

...a magic trick involves disguising a real causal sequence (e.g., a rabbit is placed in the hat when the audience is looking elsewhere) and presenting instead an apparent causal sequence (i.e., a nice floppy-eared bunny is extracted from an empty hat). The magician creates the illusion by managing events so that the apparent causal sequence is far more conspicuous than the real one. The experience of conscious will is a comparable illusion produced by the perception of an apparent causal sequence relating one's conscious thought to one's action. In reality, this may not be the causal mechanism at all.

The experience of will is the way our minds portray their operations to us, then, not their actual operation.[72]

Although the science behind it is new, the basic ideas are not. British poet and writer Samuel Johnson (1791) stated, 'All theory is against the freedom of the will, all experience is for it.'[73] We *feel* like we are exercising free will partly because we do not have good conscious access to all of the things that have shaped our preferences. The great 20th Century psychologist B.F. Skinner—who described the operant conditioning processes discussed in Chapter 4—realized that the vast amount of our behaviour is due to our past experiences, learning, and conditioning. When asked where that leaves free will, he responded:

It leaves it in the position of a fiction. We have assumed somehow or other that these internal states, feelings, and so on have initiated something, they have started something ... we have done something in a voluntary way, we have will to act. If you now look at the actual history, we find that there are external reasons why this has happened. In other words, by discovering the causes of behaviour, we can dispose of the imagined internal cause. We dispose of free will as an American Divine of the 18th Century, Jonathan Edwards, did. He said, 'We believe in free will because we know about our behaviour but not about its causes.' ... It's the object of a science of behaviour to discover causes, and once you have found those causes, there is less need to attribute to an internal act of will, and eventually I think we need to attribute nothing to it.[74]

I do not like to disagree with the eminent professor Skinner, but I believe he goes too far in claiming that we have no free will at all. Nonetheless, our *experience* of free will is not the same thing as our actual free will. Most of the things that feel like us, who we are—our likes, our dislikes, our preferences, our personalities, our mannerisms, and our habits—are due to our past experiences, what we were rewarded or punished for, what other people wanted and manipulated us to do, what situational constraints existed, and all the other interconnected and unseen causes and conditions.

When confronted with a choice, we usually pick the thing we would prefer. *This is not free will!* This is being propelled by our prior conditioning, especially if we do not stop to think about why we are choosing the thing we know we would usually always choose. Yet, if asked whether we made that choice out of our own free will, we would claim that of course it was our free will. This is because we cannot see or remember all of the past conditioning that made it highly likely we would make this exact choice now.

Experts in ancient Greek culture say that people back then didn't see their thoughts as belonging to them. When ancient Greeks had a thought, it occurred to them as a god or goddess giving an order. Apollo was telling them to be brave. Athena was telling them to fall in love. Now people hear a commercial for sour cream potato chips and rush out to buy, but now they call this free will. At least the ancient Greeks were being honest.[75]

Let me be clear. None of this research demonstrates that humans do not have free will. It demonstrates that it isn't what our phenomenological experience believes it to be. Our experience feels like our thoughts cause our actions, and although that perhaps sometimes may be true, studies show that it probably is not accurate much of the time. Our experience feels like when we make a choice, it is free will. But now it is clear that if you chose the thing that you already knew you would choose, it is not free will, but simply going along with past conditioning and habit energy.

The human brain is finely tuned to detect apparent causality from the things we see, think, and do. It is often correct. Imagine if we never learned to detect the link between hearing a growl and recognizing that the sound is causally linked to a dangerous animal. We would not have survived as a species. Our brains are constantly searching for connections between things, as this helps us to survive and to be effective. Because it does this so naturally, we do not question it, and we believe that we understand how our thoughts cause our actions.

Let's return now to karma, the actions that beget reactions. We can see from the scientific literature described above that our past actions and the resulting reactions condition our future actions. Some of this conditioning is easy to overcome and some of the habits get deeply entrenched, whether these are habits of mind, of emotion, preferences, etc.

Imagine a ball sitting in a field. As you look out across the field, you see where the land makes little hills and valleys. As the ball rolls forward, it may go down into one of the valleys. As it travels, there will be places where the valley splits, with some deeper or steeper than others.[76]

In this classic analogy, the developing person is like the ball, rolling in one direction or another.[77] At the beginning, we may have a relatively flat and open horizon in front of us, but as we make choices, we start to move in one direction rather than in another, and we gain momentum in that direction. The valleys can either have shallow or steep sides, making it easier or harder to change direction once we've gone in a certain way. This is the power of habit. It is a deep valley with steep sides, and is very hard to get out of in order to have true freedom of action. This was originally called 'canalization', as if we dig canals of different depth when we practice some attitudes or behaviours.[78] It fits very well as an intuitive analogy for how some choices put us on a path that is harder to change than others, and require more energy to change. Furthermore, it fits well with modern neuroscience. As one of the world's top developmental neuroscientists, Dr. Megan Gunnar Dahlberg, once said to me, 'Everyone thinks brain science is difficult. I can explain it in seven words. The brain becomes what the brain does.' That is, the more we practice something, we dig deeper grooves, making the sides of the canal so steep that there is almost no way for us to do anything other than what we have always done. The irony is that we believe that this is free will.

CHAPTER 11: Where Free Will Is

Have you noticed that you often have the same argument over and over again with a partner, parent, or co-worker? What's interesting about this is that if I asked you whether you *want* to have the same argument time and time again, you would likely say definitely not. Yet, it keeps happening. That's interesting ... it's against your will, yet you seem unable to stop it.

Have you ever found yourself experiencing the same types of disappointments over and over? Again, if asked whether you want that, you would say no. In Buddhist terms, this is a pretty clear example of the wheel of *Samsara*, the going round and round, and continuing to suffer. We often talk about our experience this way, of being stuck and just spinning our wheels. We seem to keep getting into the same bad situations repeatedly, despite our best and repeated intentions to break the cycle. Why?

As is likely apparent by this point, it's because of our past conditioning, our habits, and our karma—the results of our past actions. Humans are so good at learning that our reactions easily become automatic, and we don't really need to think or be present to act. This keeps us locked in a cycle of habitual automatic responses. Simply being aware of our habitual patterns, however, is not usually sufficient to break free of them. Buddhist practitioners often talk about the 'gap' in which there is freedom, but what is this gap, and where can we find it?

On many different occasions, the Buddha discussed how our actions condition future actions, and how our and others' actions are links in a chain of conditioned actions and reactions. The teaching framework is known as the Twelve Nidanas, or the twelve links in the chain of dependent arising.[79] We'll discuss all twelve in a different chapter, but let's start by examining just a tiny part of our reactions in detail.

Our experience of our lives moves so quickly that we often miss lots of what is truly going on, both inside and outside of ourselves. Let's slow things down. Consider a time someone close to you became angry with you. Perhaps you said something, teased a friend, trying to be funny, but your friend got angry instead. Perhaps a partner shared anger at feeling unappreciated. In response, a physical and emotional feeling arises, just at a gut level. Very quickly, however, you also have the desire to act. Maybe you feel ashamed and want to get away. Maybe you feel angry and want to attack. Very quickly after this, you might do something in reaction to your desire to change the situation. You leave the room or you say something sarcastic. In the framework of the Twelve Nidanas, these are steps 7, 8, and 9—typically called feeling, desire or thirst, and grasping. This is where we can have the greatest free will. To do it, however, we have to begin to pay very fine attention to our minds.

For example, the first time I helped to lead a weekend meditation retreat, I was giving a lesson on the Twelve Nidanas. We were discussing topics similar to this book, such as our reactions and free will. It was not a weekend about trauma. Nonetheless, there was one woman who had not said much during the weekend, and on the final day, we had an open session to discuss what we had learned and how we might use it as we go back to our daily lives. This woman finally spoke up, saying that she had come this weekend because her son was a drug addict and would be dead within two weeks, and she was trying to find a way to be okay with that.

I happened to be in the teacher's seat at that moment, and time slowed to a stop for me. I was terrified. She had just opened up her chest, removed her heart, and handed it to me, and was begging me to hand it back in a little better condition than it was. With one clumsy word, I could damage her more. I am not a trained therapist, and do not know how to work with pain of this magnitude.

Nonetheless, I noticed that immediately upon her speaking, I wanted to give an answer. This is simply habit energy – you ask me a question, I should answer. This is my karmic momentum built up from years of being a professor. I had learned to immediately try to answer any question put to me. But this karmic learned habit energy has no wisdom. I was just wanting to answer reflexively, but I had nothing to say, so that's a bad reason to answer. I kept silent.

The next thing I noticed was that I wanted to answer and say something that would appear wise. Oh, that's a *really* bad reason to speak! That's just my ego trying to bolster itself, and the odds that I would say something that damaged her were probably very high. I kept silent.

Finally, I realized I had something that might be helpful to say, and that's when I allowed myself to speak. I believe that all of these three stages happened in under a second, but I really don't know because I was so scared, time slowed to a crawl. It is still upsetting to me that my intention to say something helpful wasn't my first motivation, nor even my second, but my third! Ah well. Nonetheless, this ability to perceive fine grained detail of impulses in a very short time is one of the skills that can be trained through simple mindfulness meditation, and is useful for being able to see the gaps that are actually present in every moment.

When we have a strong emotional reaction to something, it typically triggers our old, learned, habitual responses. We usually do something that feels like it will make us more comfortable. This is almost always going to be a habitual response, and therefore not our free will.

If you've ever had the experience of having the rug pulled out from under you so hard that you have no idea what to do, then you were in the 'gap' that Buddhists talk about. You didn't have a preconceived or previously learned reaction. It's not always a comfortable place to be, but it is a place where you gain freedom from your past conditioning and from the wheel of samsara—the conditioned cycle of stress or suffering. You aren't spinning your wheels, having the same thing happen to you over and over again.

There is a tremendous difference between 'I don't like it' and 'It's bad', but we usually miss that difference and leap over the chasm between them. We can instead learn to take responsibility for our emotions and our reactions. This immediately gives us more control than we had when we were saying things like, 'You made me angry.' That statement is blaming someone else for your anger. The anger is yours. Own it.

Anger arose, probably because you didn't get what you wanted. That's your issue. As long as you blame the other person for your emotions, you remain a slave to the situation and to your prior conditioning.

I do not mean to say with this example that there are not valid reasons for being angry. Anger often clearly sees that something is wrong, harmful, or unjust. Nonetheless, we have to take responsibility for how we respond. If we simply blame the other person or the situation, we are less likely to find a skilful way to work with the situation.

We can train ourselves to use a strong feeling as a trigger to pay better attention to what is going on. When we feel anger, for example, we can use that strong feeling as the signal to stop spinning out the story and to step into the gap and just explore the feeling. Similarly, we can use our experience of craving and desire, and the dissatisfaction (*dukkha*) that comes from it, to be a clue to be mindful—sitting in that gap, just experiencing the craving and letting go of the need to 'do' something about it. This disrupts the karmic momentum, it impedes the habit energy. We step off of the wheel in that moment. This is Nirvana. This is what meditation can train over time—first the noticing, and second the ability to stay with your experience without pushing it away, pulling it closer, acting on it, or spacing out.

I find that, surprisingly, it's harder to stay in the feeling with good feelings than with bad feelings, because we don't really notice them as easily as bad feelings, and because we haven't much motivation to stop the thirst. It's very easy to move from feeling to craving when the experience is calm, peaceful, or pleasant. Neutral feelings are also tricky because they provide no motivation to change them, unlike unpleasant feelings which we try to get away from.

Regardless, there are at least two places where we can 'step into the gap' and break out of our habitual patterns if we want to. We'll discuss them in detail in Chapter 13, but first let's return to Diane's story to see how she found her freedom.

CHAPTER 12: Diane Shows Us How

After Diane told me about all the things she tried to do to fix her relationship with David, I felt pretty grim. She kept coming back to bang her head against what seemed like an immovable wall. Even though David seemed to want their relationship to be different, he never seemed to be willing to work with her. Rather than working to meet her halfway, David seemed to be constantly trying to control her, to fit her into some idea he had of what she was supposed to be like.

'He kept telling me that I wasn't the same as I was when I was twenty.' She rolled her eyes. 'I should certainly hope not.'

'Yeah, but how did you deal with that?'

She thought for a few moments. 'Well, you know that I don't consider myself to be a Buddhist.' I nodded. 'Nonetheless, several Buddhist practices have been very helpful for me, both throughout those difficult times and since.' She leaned forward as she considered how to explain it to me. It seemed to me like she got more solid, more real, but also lighter and more buoyant at the same time.

'I guess you'd say that I did two types of practices. First, I began to pay attention to the patterns we had, and tried not to do anything to strengthen it. We had gotten really stuck. I felt like I always knew what he was going to do or say, and I knew what I wanted to do or say. I started to see how we had gotten here. I didn't know what to do to fix it, but I could at least not add to it. I didn't need to keep being so predictable, and I certainly didn't need to react to every provocation. All I could do is work with each little thing.

'For example, I realized that if I walked into the house angry, he would simply walk away and refuse to talk to me for a week. I certainly had the right to be angry, but he couldn't hear it. His pattern was he only wanted our interactions to fit within a very narrow framework.' She paused. She blinked as tears came to her eyes. 'Once I realized that, I was so sad for him. He had closed off so much of his world, trying to get things to be just the way he wanted, that now he couldn't do what might get him what he wanted.' She wiped away a tear. I waited.

'By that point, he was working so hard to get control of everything. It ironically helped me to see what control I had. I could pay close attention to what was happening in the moment, what exact situation I was in, what the momentum was.'

'What do you mean by that?' I asked.

'Oh, I suppose lots of things. I could see patterns repeating themselves. I could remember how some particularly bad conversations had made us both hypersensitive now. I could see how the ways I had reacted in the past had sometimes reinforced his ways of behaving. I could sense that he not only had a goal for what he wanted, but he also thought he knew how I was going to act and react. I could feel my body tense up in anticipation of things he might say or do, even though he hadn't done them yet.'

I nodded. 'Yes, I've seen that in my relationships too sometimes.'

'I saw that the way I talked about the situation to myself or to others changed what options were available to me. If I thought of myself as the 'victim,' then I immediately felt powerless and angry.

'Once I began to pay attention in this way, it lessened some of the tension to need to protect myself or to react in the ways I used to. I could start to sense the freedom that is always present, even when we feel most trapped. I didn't have to try to control anything. Once I realized that, then ironically I had all the control I wanted.'

'David might say something harsh and I would feel myself clench up, I would feel like I wanted to say something mean in response, or burst into tears. Those feelings were my teachers. They became so strong or so startling that I would just notice them. I didn't need to push them away, nor did I need to indulge them. I could be aware of them. They were telling me something useful about what my prior conditioning was and what I wanted in that moment.

'It's helpful to realize it's not just about your individual actions. You have to understand why you're in the situation you're in, and work with that. You have to understand the history of the relationship you're in. Once you're clear about the situation and relationship, then you can see what actions are likely to be most beneficial.

'This is what I like about Buddhist teachings, even though I'm not Buddhist—they're very practical. They reinforce how important it is to be present with what is, not how we wish they were or how they should be. You have to work with whatever is happening at the time and not hold a grudge.'

'Isn't that like giving him a free pass to keep being an asshole?'

'No. It's the only way to have a chance to actually make things better. I could accept what was happening at the time and work with what was there, yet still know that it was wrong. If he wouldn't talk to me for a week, then that's how he's being. But if I'm still holding a grudge when he started talking to me again, then I've missed the opportunity to connect with him. Part of being present is knowing it's wrong, but being able to work with it without making things worse.'

'How do you do that?'

'We all have wisdom and clarity, but we get so hung up on what we want things to be like that we miss seeing where we can be effective. When he would stop talking to me, I could know the way he was acting was not okay. I can think about what I can do to change my actions and to try to improve the relationship. Once he started talking to me again, I could work with that. When I can change the situation, I change it. I don't keep blaming myself over it. I can only be responsible for my actions and reactions, and work to make things better.'

'Did it work?'

'No. He never took the responsibility for his actions. He just complained that I wasn't the same as I was when I was twenty. He never wanted anything to change, I guess.'

'How did you decide to leave?'

'I don't know. For a long time, I wished he would just hit me. I'd think, "Would you please just hit me so that I'd have a valid reason to leave?" It hurt so much.

'I finally got tired of being alone, being a single mother with a cold roommate, even though he was right there. There was a point where I couldn't do it anymore. I had done everything I could, but in a relationship, you have to be open to each other, you have to be willing to work together, and he just checked out, told me I had to fix everything. He never understood that it couldn't be fixed by only one person.'

She smiled warmly, which surprised me. 'I don't fault him. It's a common story. People get married young and don't grow in the same direction. He wanted things to be a certain way. We didn't know how to communicate about it. We were young and stupid.'

'What would you want to tell your younger self or someone else going through difficult times?'

'Well, I don't want anyone to think that divorce is the answer. That's not the moral of this story.'

'What is?'

'We can only ever work with what is in front of us. We are influenced by others, and they are influenced by us. Therefore, we have to be careful with our actions, including what we say or don't say. We need to be aware not only of what we're feeling, but why we're feeling it. We all carry baggage from past relationships, past moments in the present relationship, and all the other things that affect us in our lives. We may not be able to change that, but we don't need to let it control us. If we're mindful, we will have the best opportunity to have a positive influence at the right time. We have to take responsibility for our own happiness, and we can do that even when we're profoundly unhappy. If we just blame the other person, then we will stay unhappy.'

Part 3: Finding Freedom

CHAPTER 13: Where Free Will Is, and How to Gain It

Up to this point, we've recognized that karma isn't some cosmic balancing of good and bad. Good people don't just have good things happen to them. Bad actions don't always 'get what they deserve'. It is how our actions and reactions condition our future selves. It is how our past learning makes it harder to be open to what is here and now, because we begin to have expectations. I have argued that learning is another word for karma. We begin to pay attention only to particular things and want only specific outcomes. We strategize how to get things to be just the way we want. I would argue that strategy is also another word for karma.

Once we learn to pay attention, we can see the situation for what it is. Why are we in this situation? What are the forces (expectations, biases, strategies) that are shaping the momentum of the situation? What old feelings or patterns are being triggered? Once we see this, we can begin to work with it in new ways—to not be controlled by our learning, conditioning, or karma.

But we've also learned in the past chapters that free will isn't what we feel it is. If we're just reflexively trying to get more of what we like and less of what we don't, then we're not acting freely at all. We're still being controlled by our past conditioning. Where is our actual free will and how can we learn to recognize it?

Figure 9: Yama holding the wheel of becoming and rebirth. The Twelve Nidanas
are represented as the outer ring of the circle.
Source: Wikimedia Commons

The Twelve Nidanas

The Twelve Nidanas are a traditional Buddhist teaching framework, often used to describe the cycle of existence at both macro (across a whole life or multiple lives) and micro levels (at this present moment). I have found this framework to be very useful for understanding where I get stuck and how to find spaciousness and freedom. There is no need to memorize all of the details, but I believe it is helpful to have a big picture overview.

Nidana is a Sanskrit word that can be translated as a cause, or a chain that links things together, creating a chain reaction. The twelve are not truly linked in a linear chain, but it's useful to start by considering how each step conditions the next one following it. They are traditionally taught as belonging to three life periods, the past (Steps 1 and 2), the present (Steps 3–10), and the future (Steps 11 and 12), showing how our past conditions our present, which conditions our future, and the wheel keeps spinning. To reiterate, although they are typically taught in a linear fashion, as they will be here, they aren't truly linear. They can influence each other across the circle in reciprocal relationships. They are, however, largely automatic and mechanical—they are the power of habit. This wheel continues round and round, and there are very few ways to slow or stop it.

For understanding free will, Steps 6 through to 9 are the most interesting, but let's see how we get to them.

Recall that the feeling of being stuck and going round and round is called the wheel of *samsara*. The beginning of this samsara cycle is ignorance or *avidyā* in Sanskrit. In Buddhism, there is no particular concept of sin. The root of all suffering is ignorance, but of what are we ignorant? The core ignorance is separating self from other, believing that we are separate. We see ourselves as apart rather than among. Traditionally, we also do not understand our own suffering, how we make things worse, or how we could stop. Ignorance is therefore not stupidity, it is completely believing in our own ideas and the labels we project onto the world. Because of this basic ignorance, it is difficult to see one's own mind, feelings, and behaviours clearly.

Figure 9.1: Step 1—Ignorance
Source: Wikimedia Commons

Each of the Twelve Nidanas has an image that represents it. Ignorance is represented traditionally as a blind grandmother. This symbolizes the older generation, the past, which gave birth to the present situation. She is blind, however, and cannot see what is truly present, so she relies on her concepts about things. Like an older person stuck in her ways, she isn't trying to be unkind, but believes she knows what is right for you, despite not really being able to see the full picture. Nonetheless, she is inquisitive, which is the co-emergent basic intelligence that is also present in every situation—we are not doomed to always stay ignorant.

Figure 9.2: Step 2—Karmic Formations
Source: Wikimedia Commons

The image for the second Nidana is the potter's wheel, turning constantly and beginning to produce something, as this is the beginning of karma—how our past learning gives shape to our emerging present. This stage is called *saṃskāra* in Sanskrit, which is sometimes translated as karmic formations, volitional actions, that which puts together, or the karma of previous intentional actions. These karmic formations are a predisposing or shaping factor—they give ignorance its shape, power, and direction. Returning to a previous metaphor, you can think of a ball rolling down channels with a momentum previously created, with ripples up ahead that it will catch up with.

These first two Nidanas are generally considered to be past moments that give rise to the present moment. Both are therefore classified as causes of the present. The clay on the pot could be shaped into anything, but if in the prior moment, our ignorance expressed itself in terms of anger, we will create causes in a different direction than if our ignorance was expressing itself in terms of greed. In Diane's story in the previous chapter, she noticed that if she had been thinking of herself as the victim, then she became powerless. This pattern of thinking created the reality that followed.

Figure 9.3: Step 3—Rebirth Consciousness
Source: Wikimedia Commons

The third Nidana is Rebirth Consciousness or *Vijñāna*. Ignorance, the original cause of separation from the whole, merges with samskara, the seeds planted by past actions or ripples, to generate the conditions for consciousness—the basic sense of 'I am.' At this stage it is not particularly individuated and specific, but is general awareness and sometimes has been considered as including the collective unconscious. The image associated with this Nidana is a busy monkey, leaping from one thing to another.

Figure 9.4: Step 4—Name and Form
Source: Wikimedia Commons

Once conscious of ourselves, we give ourselves 'a name and function: "I am what I am, therefore I should be called Jack or Jill."[80] This step is called Name and Form or *Nāmarūpa* in Sanskrit. Nama is not name like the one our parents gave to us, but in the sense of our individual spirits. It is the same nama as in the Yogic greeting, *Namaste*. Rupa is our physical form.[81] Together, name and form are our embodied spirit, and the image for this is a man (consciousness) in a boat (body) with four oarsmen, or sometimes two people together in a boat.

Figure 9.5: Step 5—Six External senses
Source: Wikimedia Commons

Having a body with a consciousness in it is like a house with someone inside. The house has six windows through which it can perceive things outside of itself. These are the six sense organs, or *Ṣaḍāyatana* in Sanskrit, which are the next step in the process. In Buddhist psychology, we are assumed to have the typical five (sight, hearing, taste, touch, and smell) plus mind, which can perceive thoughts. This is how the embodied consciousness can experience the world and itself. These six sense doors are open, but they are still part of the 'inside' of the house. They need an outside with which to interact.

Figure 9.6: Step 6—Contact
Source: Wikimedia Commons

Now that the psychological and physical aspects of our being are in place along with sense doors to detect things outside itself, the next stage is contact or *Sparśa*. Each sense has a corresponding object with which it can connect. The eye has contact with visible forms, the ear has contact with sounds, the tongue with tastes, the nose with smells, the body with touchable objects, and the mind with thoughts, feelings, images, and complex emotions.[82] In Buddhist psychology, the meeting of sense with an object causes a type of consciousness that is particular to that meeting. Thus we have eye consciousness, nose consciousness, etc. Coming into contact with an apple, its shape and colour arise in eye consciousness, nose consciousness perhaps registers a scent. The thinking sense may recognize it as an apple. The image associated with this stage is a couple touching.[83]

As soon as our senses come into contact with an object, we register a feeling that is related to it, called *Vedanā*. This is not a complicated feeling, but just a basic awareness of whether we like it, dislike something about it, or don't care about it, or some combination of these. It is the bare reaction before we add any story to it. This could be a sense of joy

Figure 9.7: Step 7—Feeling
Source: Wikimedia Commons

or awe at seeing a beautiful sunset, the feeling of pain at getting a finger stuck in a door, or a lack of feeling at seeing someone you don't know driving past your house. Although, thoughts may be present, it is not the content of the thoughts but a recognition of positivity, negativity, or not caring. It is the tone of the thoughts and the experience, rather than the story. It is sometimes an excellent meditation practice to become aware of the feeling of your thoughts, as thoughts feel pleasant, unpleasant, or neutral. The image associated with *Vedanā* is my favourite—a man with an arrow in his eye. The image doesn't mean that contact with the world is necessarily painful, but that raw unfiltered contact with the world is jarring. It is sharp, shocking, incomprehensible, and beyond cognitive categorization.

It is said that the tone that accompanies contact is choiceless, being the result of past karma, learning or conditioning. There is some scientific evidence that supports the idea that feelings are automatically attached to perceptions of things. Passers-by at the Grand Central Terminal in New York City were asked to rate how morally 'good' or 'bad' seventy different objects were. As might be expected, some objects such as heroin and AK-47 machine guns were labelled as clearly bad and others, such as car seats for children and smoke detectors, were labelled as clearly good. The surprise was that everyday familiar objects that might seem to have no moral quality like a refrigerator or a desk were not rated as neutral—they were rated as morally good.[84] Thus, we seem to automatically attach basic feelings of good or bad to almost everything with which we come into contact.

This result demonstrates to me that not only do we attach basic feelings to the objects of our experience, but that the feeling is conditioned by our previous karma, causes, and conditions. Up through the Nidana of feeling, therefore, we have no ability to control anything because they are the result of our past conditioning. Steps 1 through 7 are all automatic processes in this framework. Buddhist teacher Reggie Ray puts it this way:

> The preceding nidanas are all 'karmic result' in the sense that they are the natural and unavoidable result of the multiplicity of past causes and conditions that are now coming to fruition. The karmic result nidanas provide the 'givenness' of our lives over which we have no control. In this important sense, these nidanas are all morally neutral.'[85]

This runs somewhat counter to the way of thinking cultivated by the Abrahamic traditions, where having a negative thought can be seen as a sin in itself. Furthermore, although a given bad or painful situation may be the result of prior karma or actions, the current situation is always karmically neutral. '... while present pain is the result of previous negative actions, its appearance at this moment is neutral and in and of itself generates no future karma. The karmic implications of past karma ripening in the present depend entirely on how we respond to it.'[86]

Nidanas 3 through 7 are seen to be the effect of prior causes, the result of prior karma, actions or learning. This changes in the next steps, where how we react to our engagement with the world can create new or intensified karmic momentum. More importantly, Nidanas 8 and 9 can either be automatic, habitual processes or intentional ones.

The 8th Nidana is *Tṛṣṇā*—desire, craving, or thirst for something. Not simply content to allow ourselves to have a feeling, we spin out some kind of story in which we enter into a personal relationship with the object. We see a co-worker, a feeling of dislike arises, and we worry

Figure 9.8: Step 8—Thirst
Source: Wikimedia Commons

about what being near this person will mean for us. We usually assign ourselves some type of role in this relationship, such as the central hero or victim.

We like the thing, experience, person, idea, and so we seek more. We dislike it, and we seek to get away from it, or harm it. We don't care about it, and so we ignore it and stop paying attention. The image associated with it is drinking something sweet and wonderful. In such a situation, we often don't take just one sip and allow the sensations to play themselves out till the end. We want more, and we want it now! We dislike this person, and we want them to go away from us as soon as possible. It is worth noting that *tṛṣṇā* was singled out by the Buddha as the primary cause of suffering and discontent—what he called the second Noble Truth. He also noted that it was not inevitable—that it could be stopped—so we are not doomed to stay stuck in this cycle. Nonetheless, the Twelve Nidanas show us the typical way most people react, our habitual response cycle. Breaking the cycle is, therefore, not necessarily easy or intuitive.

One additional reason it is not intuitive is because our culture reinforces exactly the opposite messages. You are suffering, and the solution is to give in to your cravings, to 'care' for yourself by buying things. When you disagree with something or someone, it is your 'free speech' to say your harsh opinion or snarky comments. We're taught that giving in to these desires will make us happier. The happiness purchased in these ways, however, is always fleeting. Even getting what we truly want usually causes some discomfort. We get the fancy car we've always wanted, and now we worry incessantly that it might get scratched in a parking lot, or that our neighbours are going to be envious, etc.

Although the Twelve Nidanas are typically taught in a linear fashion, one after the other, they are not intended to be understood as solely linear. Consider, for example, how feelings sometimes do not lead to craving and hunger. If you see someone suffering, such as a homeless person lying on the sidewalk, the feeling (*vedana*) it evokes is likely to be negative. The habitual reaction to negative feelings is to get away, and so we might look away from the homeless person. This is not a necessary reaction. One could instead have a feeling of compassion. A habitual reaction to something like a particularly delicious piece of cheesecake might be to get the second bite ready before we have finished chewing and swallowing the one we already have. In contrast, our reaction could be to want to share the wonderful taste with others. Feeling does not necessarily lead to thirst, but feeling coupled with attachment and conditioned by ignorance does. Thus, the different Nidanas can influence each other across the circle, although they typically follow each other due to habitual momentum.

Once we thirst to get more of something or get away from it, the craving often intensifies to become grasping or clinging, or *Upādana*. These are the actions, including mental actions, we take beyond simply daydreaming about how we want things to be different. It is the beginning of the crystallization of beliefs—I am a democrat, I am a victim, I hate him, she *always* does that, etc. In this stage, we completely identify with the object of our desire, basing our 'self' in relation to the 'other.' The image associated with grasping is a greedy person gathering as much as he or she can.

Both thirst and grasping are actions, one more mental and one more likely to be verbal or physical, but they both are the types of actions that will plant a karmic seed and start a karmic ripple. Simply thinking is a learning trial that makes thinking it again or acting on it more likely in the future. A seed has been planted. When your annoying mother says the thing she always says and you snap at her, you have dropped the rock that will cause a ripple. This is the 10th Nidana—becoming, or *Bhava* in Sanskrit. The sense of self grows in relation to the grasping. We identify with the focus of our grasping and the meaning we attribute

Figure 9.9: Step 9—Grasping
Source: Wikimedia Commons

to it. This is one more learning opportunity where we've strengthened a habit. Whether or not we were successful in grasping the desired outcome or pushing away the unwanted situation, our sense of being someone who likes or dislikes these things and situations is reinforced.

Figure 9.10: Step 10—Becoming
Source: Wikimedia Commons

If we are successful, then we've been reinforced, which strengthens the habit even more.

Imagine how that sense of a belief about ourselves helps us to become the someone we have started to believe in (e.g., 'This is how victims feel and react,' 'This is what I have to do every time to feel okay.'). The real problem is not whether our belief is correct or not. The problem is that it becomes a self-fulfilling prophecy. We begin to become the victim, the addict, or whatever role we've assigned to ourselves.

These three Nidanas, craving, grasping, and becoming have a feeling of restlessness (*dukkha*) at their core—it makes us feel that this moment isn't good enough and something needs to be added or changed. The image associated with becoming is either a couple making love or a pregnant woman, where the seed has already been planted and is growing into a recognizable form.

Figure 9.11: Step 11—Birth
Source: Wikimedia Commons

The 11th Nidana is birth/rebirth or *Jāti*, and is symbolized by a woman giving birth. Taking the mental and/or physical actions in Steps 8, 9, and 10 cause the effects in Steps 11 and 12. You are reborn as a new you, having changed yourself in some way (which may be by reinforcing an existing habitual reaction to make it stronger). Having identified our sense of self with our likes and dislikes, we act in accordance with our new or stronger belief about a self. We are angry, we are a victim, we are scared, we are a smoker, we are guilty, we are confident, etc. We give birth to this new (or reinforced) self, beginning a new karmic cycle based on this defined self, which is just another manifestation of ignorance. This perpetuates the cycle of suffering (*samsara*), setting us up for another go around the wheel.

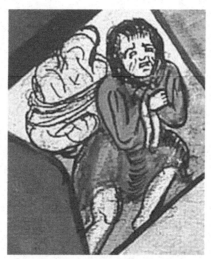

Figure 9.12: Step 12—Old Age and Death
Source: Wikimedia Commons

The final step is old age, decay, and death or *Jarāmaraṇa*, which is directly conditioned by birth. The image is carrying a corpse. Everything that has a beginning must have an end. This can be, and often has been, taken as a theory of rebirth after physical death, but I find it more useful to think of it as the death of this moment or episode, allowing the space for the next moment to arise. That next moment, however, has been conditioned by the prior ones, and so the full cycle begins again.

Putting it Together

This model is useful for understanding why you do the same things over and over again, even while claiming that you do not want to. Your habits, your conditioning, the conditioning of everyone else who expects you to act in a certain way, etc. all come together in this moment and spin with ever stronger momentum, each time continuing to reinforce the pattern. In a sense, it is entirely mechanical—it's just the way karma works when combined with human ignorance. So, does this mean that we have absolutely no free will? No. Just the opposite, actually.

This framework makes it clear exactly where we can exercise free will. There are only two places.

Steps 1 through 7 are outside of our control, they are automatic processes based on our past conditioning. For example, consider how light, your eye, your optic nerve, and your brain work automatically to see colours, shapes, edges, surfaces, and corners. You have no control over those processes; but once you see the object, such as an attractive

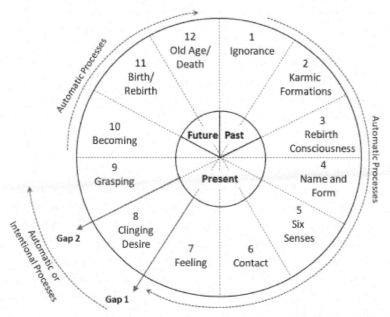

Figure 10: The Twelve Nidanas, or links in the chain of conditioned co-arising

person, and have a feeling about him/her, now you can consciously recognize the feeling (Step 7), and allow it without turning it into a craving or pushing away (Step 8). This is typically where people claim there is a 'gap' into which we can step.

I believe there is a second gap between craving (Step 8) and grasping (Step 9; see Figure 10). I may recognize that I am attracted to something (feeling, Step 7) and that I really want to get closer to it (craving). I do not have to take any actions or make any plans (grasping) based on my craving, but can just allow the feeling of desire to be as it is.

Diane described this process in her experience in the previous chapter. She said, 'David might say something harsh and I would feel myself clench up, I would feel like I wanted to say something mean in response or burst into tears. Those feelings were my teachers. They became so strong or so startling that I would just notice them. I didn't need to push them away, nor did I need to indulge them. I could be aware of them.'

This describes very nicely using the feeling in Step 7 as a trigger to step into the gap (Gap 1 in Figure 10). When she had the feeling, she didn't need to do anything other than feel it. The cycle of *anger—decide it is unfair—want to retaliate—say something unhelpful in response* was broken. Just being aware of her experience, Diane found a spaciousness in a situation that previously had felt claustrophobic and trapped.

Perhaps we miss this gap, and we move on to craving—wanting things to be different—there is still another opportunity to exercise free will. Once we feel hurt or angry (Step 7), and we want to stop feeling that way or we want to retaliate (Step 8), we can still stop ourselves from acting—we can step into the gap between craving and grasping, between the story and taking an action (Gap 2 in Figure 10). Diane described this when she said, '… if I'm still holding a grudge when he started talking to me again, then I've missed the opportunity to connect with him. Part of being present is knowing it's wrong, but being able to work with it without making it worse.' In this statement, she clearly has had an angry feeling, knows that his ignoring her is not ok, but she doesn't need to act out because of it. She can allow the feeling and her judgment, but not let that compel her to a habitual reaction.

Diane exercises true free will here, true self-control. Years of negative patterns had become habitual and entrenched, yet, she didn't let the habits control her. She also said, 'We all carry baggage from past relationships, past moments in the present relationship, and all the other things that affect us in our lives. We may not be able to change that, but we don't need to let it control us. If we're mindful, we will have the best opportunity to have a positive influence at the right time.'

We will continue to feel the weight and momentum of the past push against us. We will like some things and dislike others, based on our past conditioning. We will feel like we need to protect parts of us that were damaged previously. We may feel like we want to strike out, to regain control. Ironically, this is not control, it is being controlled by the energy of our past habit, our karma, our strategies.

So, what do we do when we have those difficult feelings? We do what Diane did. Recognize them. Feel them. And leave it at that, at least until it becomes clear that there is something useful you can do. Many times, just letting things be as they are, without trying to change them, is sufficient to change them. If nothing else, it changes you. It undermines the years of learning and habit energy that kept you locked in your pattern. It gives you the freedom to begin to try new things and make different, more positive habits.

Chögyam Trungpa described the gap in this way:

> ... nowness is not a point of reference. Nowness is what certain tantric teachings talk about as 'the fourth moment'—a state which transcends past, present, and future. So, there's no reference point at all; we are just simply being right there. The only effect is that we can afford to be open, we can afford to forget the threat. We don't have to repeat memories of the past or projections of the future. We could just be open and straightforward. At this point, the meditator sows no seed of karma for a moment; and the impulse begins to come back to sow some seed, further seeds; but then again, there's another moment that one sows no seed. There's constantly a gap which boycotts the karmic force, and then the karmic force comes back; both the non-planting force and the karmic force keep

coming back again and again. So, we are planting all the time, sowing seeds all the time, but as we begin to see the newness, we begin to sow fewer seeds of anything. That becomes more and more definite, and there are more and more gaps; there is more and more space.[87]

How can we learn to step into the gap? First, we usually need to learn to see where it is. The problem is that the links in the Twelve Nidanas move very quickly. All twelve can happen in under a second, so it appears that there is no space between them. I recall that Chögyam Trungpa said that each of the links aren't actually connected as a chain is, but that they are pushed up next to each other tightly. With practice, however, they can move slower, and the gaps between them can be stretched. Meditation can help us see the workings of our minds and habit energy with more minutely.

We can—as Diane did—use our feelings and our craving to trigger a beneficial response. Usually, when we feel a strong attraction or repulsion, although we notice the feeling, we accept it as if it is telling us something important about the world outside of us. Yet, it's just your reaction, and has no inherent truth or importance.

Buddhist philosophy and Karmic theory do not say that everything is predestined, nor that everything that happens to you is your fault. It is, instead, a deeply positive soteriological philosophy that says you do not need to stay stuck, and that you have full agency to change your life and stop suffering. It says that we have free will, but that our free will is not unlimited. There are specific places and times when we can exercise our free will.

Notice a critical aspect that this teaching demonstrates clearly—trying to get more of what we want and less of what we don't is *not* free will. It is just going along with our existing habit energy. In terms of the model, it is having the initial good, bad or neutral feeling, wanting more or less of it or to ignore it completely, and then planning what to do to get more or less of it. Trying to get more of what we like and less of what we don't keeps us stuck in the wheel of samsara.

This does not mean we always have to do the thing we don't want to, or refuse the thing we want, although those are clearer examples of exercising free will—we're actively rejecting our habitual automatic reaction. It means that to truly exercise free will, we have to stop the process at feeling or craving, and pause there. We can examine the feeling. How are we experiencing it? What is it trying to get us to do? What motivations are there? What stories arise in reaction to the feeling? Do we believe the stories? Why do we? What action would be skilful and appropriate in this moment? What action is more likely to lead to long term contentment and benefit, both for self and others? When we step into the gap, we gain space to recognize that we do not have to do the habitual action, but can try something different. We may also find that going along with our originally desired action will be fine. The point is that if we simply do what we think we want, we are not in control of our lives, we are being controlled by our past conditioning, our past learning, our karma.

CHAPTER 14: Karma and Freedom

Honing our Discernment

How do we put all of this together? Where are karma and free will linked?

We began by recognizing that karma isn't what most people think it is. It is not a tit-for-tat balancing of the scale. If you do something good, it is not guaranteed you'd get something good. Bad things can still happen to good people. It isn't a type of predestination or fate either, where the outcome is fixed and there is nothing you can do. Instead, the best modern synonym is probably learning. We become conditioned to like some things, dislike others, care about some issues and not others, based on our experiences. We try different actions and get rewarded for some and punished for others. This changes the odds of us acting similarly in the future. This changing of odds *is* karma. We are no longer open to all possibilities. So, when we walk into a new situation, we have blinders on. We create strategies to try to get more of what we like and less of what we don't. Every strategy is our past karma influencing the present, which then sets more conditions for the future.

We similarly recognized that free will is not what most people think it is. It isn't simply doing what you like, that's you being controlled by your past conditioning. It isn't doing what feels 'natural', because what feels natural to you is also partly based on your past learning. We often feel that our thoughts are controlling our actions, but as was shown in Chapters 9 and 10, the thoughts are a result of something deeper making the decision, and then, the conscious thought arises. We get into patterns, habits of thought, habits of feeling, habits of speech and actions. When we react to situations, we believe we are acting with free will, but in fact, we're usually just running on habit energy. We have a feeling that we want something or some outcome, and we act to get it. As long as we don't pause and step into the gap between feeling and wanting, or the gap between wanting and acting, we are being impelled by our past conditioning and are, therefore, not acting from our free will. We are letting our karmic momentum push us in the direction we always go, which will likely end up having the same results it always does. We give up our agency to our old self, propelled by old fears, anxieties, hopes, and insults.

Karma pushes us to stay locked into patterns, and we take actions that feel like free will, but which actually reinforce the existing patterns. It doesn't need to be this way. Once we see that we have a pattern, we can stop letting it control us. We can use the push we feel—the karmic momentum—as the trigger to pause and reflect, to step into the gap. When we have a strong desire to have something, that feeling of desire clues us in to the fact that we're being impelled by our prior conditioning and our pre-existing ideas about desirable outcomes. When we feel like we know what action we want to take, we're feeling our karmic momentum. If we don't notice it, then we will just automatically do the thing we have been conditioned to do, which further reinforces the habit. If we do notice it, but don't pause to change the momentum, then also we are simply reinforcing our existing conditioning. If, however, we notice it, and we pause to consider whether taking the action we feel like taking will lead to long-term benefit or harm, then we are both stopping our karma and exercising our full agency.

Emotions

Typically, however, we get swept away with the emotion of the situation, especially if the situation provokes a strong reaction. If someone says something unkind to you, perhaps a sexist or racist comment, your ears come into contact with the words, and a feeling results, likely to be anger, in this case. Depending on your past history, you might be very sensitive to these types of comments and feel like lashing out and saying something unkind in return. You would likely feel justified to retaliate, as the original comment was completely unwarranted, unfair, and cruel. The pressure to react will likely be strong. Stronger pressure, however, is not a good indication of how justified you are to react. Instead, it is an excellent indicator of how strong your prior conditioning has been. The more you feel like you can't stop to pause, the more you're being controlled by your karmic momentum. If you feel like you shouldn't pause to look at what you're about to do, then you definitely should. It is your conditioning and ignorance impelling you to do what you could have guessed you would do in this type of situation because you've probably done it before.

My older daughter lived with a roommate in a tiny, one-room studio apartment during her last year of college. Her roommate, whom we'll call Greg, had been a good friend for a couple of years. She and Greg had regularly gotten together for a year to study several times a week, so they knew they'd be good roommates.

After only a couple of months together, however, little things started to annoy my daughter. 'He had his own dishes, but he kept using mine, which wasn't a big deal. But then he wouldn't wash them, and I'd have to clean up after him before I could make my dinner.

'Then he got a job where he had to get up at 3 a.m. He would slam doors and use the blender, waking me up. I would ask him politely not to run the blender if I'm asleep and to be gentle with the bathroom door. He always said yes, but the next day, he'd do the same thing. I don't think he was trying to be unkind; he just didn't think about how noisy he was.

'The thing that really pushed me over the edge, however, was the dishes. I had asked him never to use my cast iron pan. I explained that I had just gotten it seasoned perfectly and that it was not for cooking meat in.[ii] One day, I came home to find that not only had he used it, he left it in a sink full of water, and now it was all rusty. When I confronted him about it, he said he used it because his pan was dirty and he didn't want to clean it. I was furious.'

[ii] Note: My daughter is a vegetarian, but Greg was not.

'So, what did you do?' I asked.

'We usually used his utensils. Every other time I used one of his spoons, I threw it in the garbage. This was my little revenge. Over time, he started wondering where all his spoons were. Of course, this backfired because it left us with no spoons, even when I needed one.'

In this example, prior conditioning trained my daughter that when someone is routinely annoying, then she is justified to be angry and should retaliate in some way. Most of us have probably had similar experiences, where someone angers us and we feel an immediate reaction arise. When we've reacted in the past, we've probably felt a type of righteousness after saying the nasty comment—we've self-reinforced our bad behaviour, making it more likely to happen again in the future. Furthermore, we see this script all the time in movies, on TV, and in video games—someone says or does something harmful to our 'hero', who does something harmful in return. This karmic pattern is very well established, and it moves fast.

What if we insert the pause as soon as feel the impulse to retaliate? How long should the pause be? What do we do in that gap?

There isn't one 'right' answer. Buddhist teacher Pema Chödrön says that simply pausing to feel three breaths with our full intention is often enough to begin to weaken the karmic pattern. It can often be useful to place our attention on our physical feelings—what do we feel and where? We can simply wait, experiencing the play and change of our feelings as we watch them. Sometimes, a good response will appear. Sometimes it won't. You can try to consider the other person's position, to see if it helps to give additional context. You can examine what you feel like doing and try to understand why that's your go-to reaction. You can recall other times you've felt this way, how you had usually reacted, and what the outcomes were. In short, there's a lot you can do when you step into the gap, although the gap is not really about doing something, but relaxing into the situation. Nonetheless, doing anything to slow down the momentum and weaken your existing conditioning gives you more freedom to choose how to respond.

For example, if someone says something unkind, we feel the first flush of anger and we feel the impulse to retaliate. But we stop ourselves from doing it right away. We pause and examine the feeling. It's in our chest and stomach, and it feels like burning. We might consider that the other person didn't even realize why their statement might be offensive. If that's the case, maybe compassion is a better response. Perhaps, we could say something gentle to help him see how to say it differently. We might recognize that the other person is speaking from a place of pain, and again, perhaps, a kind word might soften the situation and give you the opportunity to make a friend. Or maybe you'll realize that it's important that you react strongly to show him just how offensive his statement was. The point is that there isn't only one 'right' response. If we just react, we continue being controlled by our karma, and your reaction will feel like your 'free will', but it isn't. The only way to exercise truly free will is to use the strong feeling and step into the gap between the angry feeling and the desire to react, recognize the pressures on you from your past and the situation, and then choose how to respond, instead of reacting habitually. If we're not paying attention, we zip right past the gaps and keep the cycle spinning faster and faster. If we pause briefly in the gaps, it may not change what you choose to do, but it certainly gives a better chance of a healthy outcome, and may get you a transformative outcome sometimes.

Radical Transformation is Possible

My parents got divorced when I was ten. At that time, there wasn't enough research on how best to handle divorces with children, and my parents made a lot of—what we now know are—big mistakes. It's not their fault, they didn't know better. Nonetheless, some of those mistakes had what felt like lifelong consequences. I'm not claiming that what I'm going to tell you is the exact truth, but it is what I remember.

One thing experts say is never to put the child in the middle of the arguments. My mother did that a lot. She would tell me ways that my father hurt her, and even when I screamed that I didn't want to hear it, she couldn't stop. She needed a friend, and I *had* to be that friend. Maybe she wanted me on her 'side', another thing experts say you shouldn't do. One outcome of this was that in a short time, a distance grew between us. I guess as a child I felt that she wasn't able to have my best interests at heart because of her pain. I could no longer trust her intentions or actions completely.

I don't mean to suggest that we ever had a bad relationship. As I grew up, I just always seemed to hold something back. When we would get together, it was pleasant, but I would feel like I wasn't completely accepted as myself. This came out most clearly when talking about my life, and my mother would want to give me advice. It's not that her advice wasn't kind, heartfelt, or even wise. It's just that it always felt to me like a subtle kind of attack. Why did it feel this way to me? This was my old conditioning from when I was ten, colouring my perception of her years later. She was never trying to be unkind or dismissive of me. She was intending to be helpful, but I always took it as her not accepting me.

For example, my mother tried many times to reconvert me after I left the Christian faith. My favourite of these stories is the time she gave me her personal testimonial when I was in my early 30s. We were sitting outside, on a beautiful summer day. The sun dappled through the trees, and birds chittered lightly. Nonetheless, I felt my stomach tighten immediately as she began talking.

She said, 'When I was getting divorced from your father, I had a dream, and in the dream I was in a dark basement. I was stumbling around, trying to find my way out. Finally, I found the bottom of the stairs and as I looked up I could see that the door was cracked open just a bit at the top and from behind the door was a brilliant white light. I climbed the stairs and as I neared the top, I heard a voice. The voice said, "Go out. Take only what you need. Close the door behind you."' She looked at me meaningfully. 'And that was God telling me to take what was good from my marriage, leave the rest behind, and move on with my life.'

'Wow, what a powerful, important dream that was for you!'

She scowled. 'No, no. That wasn't a dream. That was God talking to me.'

I repeated, 'Wow, what a powerful, important dream that was for you!'

'No, no, no! It wasn't a dream. I couldn't have had that dream unless God had sent it to me!'

'Look, mom, you can't expect me to believe in the Missouri Synod Lutheran God just because you had a dream,' I protested.

'Yes, I can.'

'Okay, okay,' I laughed. 'You can expect anything you want. But I didn't have that dream. I don't think I would interpret it the same way even if I had.'

There are two things I love about this moment. First, whether or not I could understand her experience, it had transformed her. From that time to the present day, she has lived her life differently. She has no doubt that there is a personal God who is paying attention to her and will step in to help, if needed. This allowed her to change her life and to trust her chosen path completely. This is exactly what a spiritual path should do and I have profound respect for that.

The second thing that strikes me is the disparity between what was really happening and what I thought was happening. At the time, I withdrew even before she started. As the conversation went on, I felt pressured and unaccepted. Yet, as I look back on it now, she was practising the very essence of kindness. She was trying to share the most important and intimate moment of her spiritual life with me. She was trying to help me to see things in a way I couldn't from my perspective. But I couldn't see or accept that because of my prior conditioning, which made me assume that she didn't accept who I was and that she wanted me to be different, to be more like her. That little sliver of lack of trust that had occurred when I was ten still controlled what I could hear, see, and accept. I was still reacting like a ten-year-old boy being told what to do.

As I said, my mother and I have always had what I would characterize as a good relationship. I just always felt a little hesitation, or held a little something back. I didn't really mind that, even once I started to understand why. I knew I had been hurt as a child and that I hadn't been fully able to trust the relationship since then. I expected it would be like this for my whole life. But miracles *can* happen.

Over time, as my Buddhist practice deepened, I didn't hide it from my mother, but neither was I overly open about it. I didn't feel like she would approve of or like it, and that she'd just want to reconvert me. Again, notice how I'm believing in a version of the world that wasn't even happening. I was projecting what she *would be like* if I talked about it. This is how karma manifests and continues itself. I wasn't really even giving her a chance to be different. I just kept expecting her to behave in a particular way and, therefore, I treated her in a way that ensured she stayed that way to me.

When I was about fifty, my parents wanted to visit me. The week they wanted to visit included a weekend where I was leading a full-day Buddhist retreat. Immediately, I felt uncomfortable. 'Are you sure you want to come *that* week? I'm going to be busy all day Saturday. Wouldn't you rather come the next week?'

I 'knew' that if they came at that time, they would ask what I was doing. I wasn't going to lie, and then it would be in their faces, and everyone would be uncomfortable. But no, that was the time they intended to visit.

They arrived on Wednesday, and just as I expected, asked me what I was doing on Saturday. I told them I was leading a Buddhist retreat and that they were welcome to come to it if they wanted. They said they had something that they wanted to do in the afternoon, but would see.

On Saturday, I got up early and went to prepare the space for the day. Just as we were about to begin, my mother and stepfather arrived and sat near the back. They stayed for the first half, leaving about lunch time. At the time, I expected a somewhat uncomfortable evening once we both got home. I certainly did not expect a complete transformation of my relationship with my mother.

When they got home, they sat in the family room with me. We asked each other about our days. They asked questions about what I had led that morning and what happened in the afternoon. We discussed the Buddhist teachings. We discussed the overlap between Buddhist and Christian teachings. I don't really remember what we talked about. What I remember is that, for the first time since I was ten, I felt seen. I felt accepted. I felt like all the forty years of mistrust completely vanished. Ever since that moment, I have felt very close to my mother again.

What changed? I don't really know. Did they get more flexible as they got older? That's not what usually happens in older age. Did they see the overlap between our philosophies and recognize that we care about the same things even though we use different words? Did they see that I was just as committed as they were, and they respected my commitment, even though it wasn't their path? I don't know.

And the reason I don't know is because every one of these questions is looking in the wrong place—each makes the assumption that *my parents* changed.

Here's what I do know. By the time I got home that evening, I was no longer worried about the conversation that might happen when they returned. I didn't set myself up to expect anything. I didn't worry about whether it would be uncomfortable. In fact, I allowed that it might be, and that would be just fine. I didn't react to my ideas about what might happen, and once the conversation began, I didn't react to any of it either. If uncomfortable feelings arose, I just let them be. I didn't try to steer the conversation to any specific outcome. I didn't worry about what any question or statement they made 'meant.' I just conversed openly and honestly. Although I didn't think of it at the time, in retrospect, it looks like I stepped into the gap and stayed there for the hour of our conversation, just allowing what was happening to go on. In doing so, I felt accepted. This completely transformed my relationship with my mother, something I never believed would happen.

When we become aware that the feelings we're having, the things we expect, and the outcomes we want are due to our past karma and conditioning, we gain the opportunity to not keep letting the cycle spin out of our control. Awareness, however, is not enough. We have to actively choose to step out of the circle into the gaps, where we gain the ability to respond rather than react. This doesn't mean we don't continue to feel the pressures, the desires, and the expectations. We feel them, but we just don't believe them in the same way. We can see that many of them are simply the result of our past learning and conditioning, and therefore, they may not be accurate in the current situation. We can, then, exercise true free will, choosing the action that seems most appropriate for the exact situation we're in, not for the similar situation we once were in. If we continue the reflexive actions, the ones that feel the most 'natural' to us, then we stay locked in the cycle of karma with little chance of changing how our lives are going.

The cycle of conditioned actions—the Twelve Nidanas—just keeps going round and round, pressing the steps closer and closer to each other. As long as it does, we have little opportunity for true agency over our lives, because we keep missing the gaps where free will can best be exercised. With practice, however, we can hone our perception, slow the wheel down, and spend more time in the spaciousness that always exists, whether we see it or not. When you act from this place, what seems like miraculous transformation is possible.

CHAPTER 15: Radical Freedom

We get stuck in habitual patterns. This habit energy controls us much of the time. Usually, we don't notice this, we just do what feels most natural. As you know by now, what feels most natural is what you've practised the most, so you are being controlled by your past. When we awaken to this, it can feel overwhelming and heavy, feeling the weight of all that karmic momentum. Nonetheless, after all of this discussion on karma, we come to the Zen punchline—karma doesn't exist. It is just a set of ideas, and although they may be useful ideas to help us see where we get stuck and how to get unstuck, they have no more reality than any other set of ideas. 'Karma possesses only relative reality by nature, and because of that, it is something we can transcend.'[88]

The truth is that, at any moment, we have radical freedom. The gap is always there, and once we step into the gap, we can go in any direction we want. Chögyam Trungpa likened karma to a game of chess, 'Your particular position at any point is determined by where you were and what your moves were; but after that point, it is up to you.'[89]

In order to use this radical freedom, we have to be awake. My definition of an awakened being is that an awakened person is one who trusts that the next moment will be workable. We spend a vast amount of time worrying about how to get more of what we want and less of what we don't. We become anxious about what might happen. We strategize about what we could do and say to influence the outcome of things that haven't happened yet. Strategy is just another word for karma. A strategy is based on what we have learned, our past conditioning, our planning, our feelings, craving, and grasping. We get into a difficult or stressful situation and we start thinking and strategizing. But it was our very best thinking that got us into this mess! As Zen Master Seung Sahn was fond of saying, 'Put it all down.'

It isn't that we are supposed to have no feelings or preferences. Trying to deny our experience and our opinions would be a form of violence on one's own self. Instead, we can recognize that we have feelings, but that they are also empty of any independent reality and they do not reflect something true about the world. They are simply our opinions and desires. When we put down our need to strategize, plan, and control, we can gain trust that the next moment will be workable. We can gain trust in ourselves as being able to handle whatever comes our way.

Diane

Recently, I met up with Diane in her favourite coffee shop. She arrived right on time, moving easily and lightly among the tables. She had remarried about five years after separating from David, and her daughter has now graduated from high school and is moving into relationships of her own.

As Diane took off her coat and sat down, she seemed much the same as she had on prior meetings. She ordered the same latte. She had the same easy grace and comfort. Her long hair fell across the predominantly earth tones wardrobe she still favoured, although the cut of clothes were looser. There were laughter lines around her eyes now, but they didn't seem to be because she was older.

After catching up for a while, I asked her to reflect on her experiences.

Diane smiled easily. 'I thought you might ask me that,' she said. 'You know, a couple of years after the divorce, my mother commented on how glad she was that I was free finally,' Diane shrugged her shoulders.

'She never understood. I was free for a long time before I finally decided to leave the marriage. I was free as soon as I stopped being controlled by my anger, my wanting things to be different, and the habitual patterns we had created.'

She took a drink and considered its feel and taste. She swallowed and continued, 'People don't understand freedom. It isn't that you like every choice you make or that you're happy about every situation you're in. It's about being content to work with what you've got in each moment. It's about feeling the various pushes and pulls on you and having the ability to choose, not simply reacting out of old damage or habit.'

I nodded. 'You can tell people that, but they don't really want to understand. They just want a magic pill to make everything happy all the time.'

'That's what keeps them stuck.'

'Yes, there's so much focus on what happened in the past and what future outcome they fear or want that they miss the freedom available to them in each moment.'

'Well, that's the tricky part, isn't it? Freedom has to be sought over and over again as the situation changes. It isn't just a thing you attain and never have to consider again.'

I smiled. 'Yes, my teacher always says that correct meditation isn't something special you do on a cushion, or at a certain time, or with special incense. He says correct meditation is maintaining your mind, moment after moment.'

Diane looked pensive as she considered that. 'I like it … maintaining your mind.' She looked around the coffee shop. There weren't too many people there that morning, despite it being clear and cool. 'What happens without proper maintenance? Everything starts to fall apart. When you stop recognizing what you're feeling, why you're in the situation, or that you're fixated on having things turn out in a certain way, then your ability to act freely is greatly hampered.' She took a sip and added, 'At least, that's my experience.'

'You seem to have come a long way.'

When I think back on those times, it's hard for me to really understand the person that I was. I wasn't happy. It felt like old baggage issues were making me try to control situations and everyone around me, and it was making me unhappy.

'I felt totally inadequate. I kept reliving all these old hurts and I never felt any better. I felt there must be something wrong with me. I thought if I just retold the stories again and again, it would make me figure out how to make me better. But it didn't.' She sighed at the memory.

'The narratives in my head kept me constantly dwelling on the past, my hurts, my disappointments, my lack of control. I made myself sick, constantly worrying about controlling the future, lying awake at night, rehashing these stories.

'I had no peace with myself. I constantly second-guessed everything. "I should have done that. I messed this up and should have continued on that path. I should have chosen this career. I'm stuck. I'm not good enough." I was constantly worried that a crisis would erupt or that he'd punish me for some tiny, little thing. I knew I couldn't continue like that.'

She sat up and leaned closer to me. 'You know,' she said almost conspiratorially, 'everyone carries the weight of the past differently, but we can learn to work with it skilfully. I was stuck, and I needed to make peace with all of it. And I did! That's the amazing part. The ability to see the moment when change can happen improved my relationship with my daughter, my marriage, and myself. Finding that has been priceless, and maybe I wouldn't have found it if things hadn't gotten so bad for a while.'

'So, I'm really grateful to David at this point. What started as him trying to control me showed me how not to be controlled by myself. That's true freedom,' she said joyfully.

Trust and Freedom

Diane learned to work with her karma, recognizing why she was in the situation she was in, and not fighting over what was in the past. She learned to work toward her desired goals flexibly, doing what she could at the times she could, not trying to force it. She learned that even her strongest, most difficult emotions could be the catalyst to free her from the habits that had previously kept her stuck. She learned to trust herself.

It is funny to me that most people don't trust themselves to be able to be okay with and work with whatever arises, because our actual, lived experience is that we always have been able to be okay. Even when we have had horrible things happen to us, we have actually been able to get through them. When we have planned and strategized for how to manipulate the situation to get a desired outcome, the conversation never went the way we had planned, and yet, we were able to adapt to the situation as it changed, maybe not gracefully, but still. So, our real-world experience is that we have always been able to work with whatever arises, but we live in a state of anxiety that, maybe, the next moment will be terrible. I have a secret for you. Even if the next moment is terrible, you can still work with it and be okay.

10th Century Ch'an Master Yúnmén was asked, 'What is the highest, most profound teaching of all the Buddhas?' He answered, 'An appropriate response.' This is perhaps my favourite kong-an (*koan* in Japanese)—an enigmatic Zen puzzle that teaches a deeper truth. What is an appropriate response? It requires being open to the moment, not having something prepared, not having a strategy. It requires being alert to the subtle and unique characteristics of the unfolding situation, the relationships that exist, and your role in the situation. It is not unaware of the past, as the history informs the situation, relationships, and function. It is not unaware of the future, as we must maintain consideration of what will lead to long-term benefit for self and others. What may be an appropriate response in this moment will be different from the next. What is appropriate in one situation is not in the next.

This kong-an tells us how to work with karma. The situation we are in, where we are physically, how others are feeling, and our history are all already determined by past actions, causes, and conditions. Yet, if we do the habitual thing, the odds of us responding appropriately are low. We are simply reacting out of our already-established patterns of habit. If, instead, we maintain awareness that this situation is unique, we will still feel the pulls of habit energy, but we have the freedom to respond appropriately.

Because everything is interdependent, karma also arises dependent upon other conditions; it lacks an inherent and independent existence. Therefore, it can be overcome. When we recognize the interconnectedness of everything and the fact that everything is as it is at this moment because of the rich interconnected set of actions, causes, and conditions that have led to this moment, we can also recognize that *everything is as it must be* at this moment. For anything to be different at this moment, some different action would have had to be taken in the past. Everything is exactly as it has to be based on all of the prior causes and conditions. The conclusion I draw from this is that everything is perfect in this moment.

This conclusion does not mean that everything is happy, that there is no injustice or pain. It simply means that the injustice, pain, happiness, and everything cannot be otherwise due to what has come before. Once we accept that, we gain the agency to do something. We cannot change anything that is, because it already is. We can only set an intention and direction to change ourselves to create a new interconnected moment that can have more contentment, compassion, and openness.

People tend to spend a vast amount of their time and energy obsessing over the past and planning for the future. Both of these keep us locked into our habitual karmic patterns, because they distract from seeing the gaps. We think we have control when we don't, such as planning future conversations or wearing a lucky shirt to help your team win; and we give up our control when we do have it, such as by reacting to the conversation habitually or believing the story we tell ourselves about what is happening.

Once we accept that everything is as it must be at this moment, there is no need to worry about the past. Once we accept that strategizing for the future is our karma controlling us, there is no need to be anxious about or plan for the future. Once we let go of the past and the future, we regain all of the energy we have been wasting. That energy is now available to the present moment, which is the only place we can respond appropriately.

Diane realized exactly this. She recognized how her marriage had gotten terribly stuck. She recognized that David's actions were harmful and unreasonable. She also realized that there was nothing she could do about any of that, so holding a grudge would only put energy into the problems, giving them even more momentum. By allowing the situation to be as it is, no mental or emotional energy was wasted on strategizing, self-justifying, anger, self-recrimination, guilt, etc. If she had spent time blaming David, her situation, herself, or anything else for that matter, that energy would not only be wasted, she would stay stuck because blame just reinforces the patterns that keep you stuck. By stepping into the gap and staying balanced, all her energy was available to act in the present situation, making it much more likely that she could actually make effective changes. She could respond appropriately to whatever the next situation offered.

CHAPTER 16: Finding Your Freedom

Diane never finished her college degree. She found that she didn't need it to be happy. She put in the practice and effort to have clarity about how her mind works. She fine-tuned her perception to recognize the old karma that put her in any given position, and to feel the impulses of her past learning. She used this clarity to not be pushed around by her past or by others, but to work with what she could. It turns out that's more than enough.

Her story is not unique. We can all regain agency and free will when we return to the present situation, relationship, and function.

Chögyam Trungpa Rinpoche said essentially the same thing in a discussion with his students:

CTR: On the whole, the karmic situation is based on your having some kind of footing in the past, which goes on indefinitely. But that doesn't dominate or control your present existence— you can make your own choice ... The past situation brought you up to this present point. Beyond that, it's up to you to relate with that particular present situation. Where you go from here seems to be purely up to you. So the sense of freedom or personal choice goes on constantly, all the time ...

Question: ... you said there was also the element of choice.

CTR: ... karma is a choiceless choice. You can't step back because there's choice; and you have to get into the heart of the choice, so it becomes a choiceless choice ...

Question: Wouldn't it take a great exercise of will to make one choice over, let's say, a familiar samsaric pattern of choice?

CTR: I don't think so, because we don't try to get out of samsaric pattern deliberately, but we try to get at what is. We could meditate every day upon samsara and upon what is liberation, freedom, the enlightened approach. But, instead, we just relate with things as they are, simply. We have no choice in that sense, we are just simply dealing with what is common sense and what is the sane approach. There's no metaphorical situation or metaphysical situation involved in that at all. [90]

So how do we learn to practise seeing and working with our karma? How do we learn to step into the gap and break free from our habitual patterns? The good news is that there are many ways.

Most of the paths use meditation as a backbone of the practice. With it, we can begin to familiarize ourselves with our habits of mind. These habits keep us stuck. We can't change a habit until we become familiar with how it manifests itself. Many meditation techniques, such as mindfulness and shamatha meditations, focus on giving us the space and stability to begin to see how our minds and emotions pull us around, controlling us because of past karma or learning.

For example, consider a simple mindfulness of breath meditation where you place your attention on your breath and try to hold it there. You will get distracted. Some of these distractions may come from outside, such as noises, the telephone, or your children walking into the room. Most of the distractions, however, will come from your own mind. That's useful information. Although any individual thought or feeling may appear random, as you gain experience, you'll begin to recognize the patterns in the types of distractions you offer yourself. You might notice particular feelings or ideas appearing repeatedly. These are often evidence of your past karma.

Once we begin to have familiarity with our mental habits, then we can work with meditation techniques that focus on cultivating new habits. Again, there are many different cultivation techniques, such as loving-kindness and tonglen, that help to break the self-centredness of our thoughts. That selfishness tends to keep us stuck, as we remain focused on getting more of what we want and less of what we don't. As has been said many times, this motivation is not free will—it's us being controlled by past karma or learning.

We can also work directly with honing our perception to notice our experiences in more minute detail. Notice, for example, how quickly we move to desire and grasping after we have a feeling. Once we begin to see our experience clearly, we have a much greater agency to step into the gap and off of the wheel of suffering.

We find we don't have to be pushed around by our habits and prior preferences. Once we enter the gap, we have true free will. That is, we might still choose to do the thing we like, but we're doing it as an active choice, not as a habitual reflex.

Can you learn and practise these techniques all by yourself? Yes. You can, however, learn them faster with the help of a qualified teacher, such as you might find at a local Zen centre or meditation group.

The Buddha changed the way people understood karma. He changed it from being a mystical force to being something rational that we can examine and test. 'He used it originally as a method for recovering humanity—for healing humanity'.[91] We can use our understanding of karma to stop blaming ourselves and others for our fates, and to find the freedom to act—to regain our agency.

The ultimate lesson of karma is that everything matters. Every thought, word, and act. We need to take responsibility for ourselves, and in so doing, we stop being victims. 'Man's present situation derives from old karma, but he remains free to make what he will of his present … What is predetermined, then, is an individual's opportunity for genuinely ethical behaviour, rather than his inner moral tendencies.'[92]

There is a tremendous amount of growing up that takes place between 'It fell,' and 'I broke it.' Taking responsibility for ourselves reduces the burden on others. This will feel uncomfortable sometimes, but that is what true agency is. When we are just doing what feels comfortable, we're acting out of habit, not free will.

This doesn't mean we have to try to stay uncomfortable. It means that we don't need to chase comfort. We don't need to keep trying to force our situation to be different. We don't need things to be a certain way to be okay. We can trust ourselves. We can be okay, no matter what. We can work with whatever our situation is. We can set intentions and aspirations for things to improve, but be entirely flexible about what that improvement looks like, and how we get there. We can work skilfully with our karma to plant seeds to make things easier for us in the future.

We can only do these things easily, however, when we're paying attention. So, working to pay closer attention is the first step. The second step is learning to allow the situation to be as it is. Old karma, the karma of result, along with numerous causes and conditions have resulted in everything that you are currently experiencing. You can't stop it, so you might as well relax and allow it. Now you regain all of your power to work with it, rather than wasting your power fighting what is.

You are enough. You always have been. May you learn to trust it.

Acknowledgements

I am immensely grateful to my daughters Lauren Evelyn and Kristin Nicole, and my wife Jennifer, who teach me daily about the importance of karma, choice, intention, responsibility, and freedom. I wish to thank all of my teachers who have shaped my thoughts, understanding, and awake moments. In particular, this project would not have been completed without the guidance and support of the Most Venerable Wonji Dharma and the Five Mountain Zen Order. I also owe much to several teachers in the Shambhala lineage, including Ethan Nichtern, Pema Chödrön, and the Windhorse Retreat Center. I am further grateful to Kim Eldredge Galloway, who helped me to write in human (as opposed to academic) language.

It is a remarkable time to be alive, where we can learn from multiple traditions of wisdom easily. This ability allows for a deeper understanding of difficult concepts, such as karma, than may have been possible previously, when one would only be exposed to a single style of teaching. It is my hope that this synthesis is helpful in liberating beings from suffering.

Notes

1 Wedekind C, Seebeck T, Bettens F, Paepke AJ. MHC-dependent mate preferences in humans. *Proceedings Biological sciences*. 1995;260(1359): 245–249.

2 Thakkar C. Karma. 2015, December 4; https://www.ancient.eu/ Karma/. Accessed September 28, 2017.

3 Kyabgon T. *Karma: What It Is, What It Isn't, Why It Matters*. Boston, MA: Shambhala; 2015, p. 15.

4 Bhikkhu T. Karma. 2011; http://www.accesstoinsight.org/lib/ authors/thanissaro/karma.html. Accessed September 28, 2017.

5 Ray R. *Indestructible Truth*. Boston, MA: Shambhala; 2002.

6 Kapleau P. *The Wheel of Death: Writings from Zen Buddhist and other Sources*. New York: Harper & Row; 1971.

7 Kapleau P. *The Wheel of Death: Writings from Zen Buddhist and other Sources*. New York: Harper & Row; 1971, p. 24.

8 Kapleau P. *The Wheel of Death: Writings from Zen Buddhist and other Sources*. New York: Harper & Row; 1971, p. 22.

9 Kyabgon T. *Karma: What It Is, What It Isn't, Why It Matters*. Boston, MA: Shambhala; 2015, pp. 113–114.

10 Shun'ei T. *Living Yogacara*. Boston: Wisdom Publications; 2009.

11 Ray R. *Indestructible Truth*. Boston, MA: Shambhala; 2002, p. 258.

[12] McDermott JP. *Development in the early Buddhist concept of kamma/karma.* New Delhi, India: Munshiram Manoharlal Publishers; 1984, p. 153.

[13] Kapleau P. *The Wheel of Death: Writings from Zen Buddhist and other Sources* New York: Harper & Row; 1971, p. 26.

[14] When asked about this, he said that for anyone who holds the view, "'Whatever a human being experiences, whether pleasure, or pain, or neither pleasure nor pain—all this is by reason of what was done in the past," **they go beyond what is personally known**, and what is considered as truth in the world. Therefore, I say … that they are wrong.' (McDermott JP. *Development in the early Buddhist concept of kamma/karma.* New Delhi, India: Munshiram Manoharlal Publishers; 1984, pp. 16–17, emphasis added.)

[15] If you would like more details about learning, see:

- Gentile DA & Gentile JR. *Learning from video games (and everything else): The general learning model.* Cambridge, UK: Cambridge University Press; 2021.
- Bandura A. Social learning theory. Englewood Cliffs: Prentice Hall; 1977.
- Gibson EJ. Principles of perceptual learning and development. In. New York: Appleton-Century-Crofts; 1969.
- Kandel ER, Kupfermann I, Iversen S. Learning and Memory. In: Kandel ER, Schwartz JH, Jessell TM, eds. Principles of neural science. 4th Ed. New York: McGraw-Hill; 2000:1227–1246.

[16] Skinner BF. *The Behavior of Organisms.* New York: Appleton-Century-Crofts; 1938.

Thorndike EL. *Animal Intelligence: Experimental Studies.* Forgotten Books; 1911.

[17] Skinner B. *About behaviourism.* Alfred A. Knopf; 1974.

[18] Amsel A. Frustrative nonreward in partial reinforcement and discrimination learning: Some recent history and a theoretical extension. *Psychological Review.* 1962;69(4):306–328.

[19] Seligman ME. *Helplessness: On Depression, Development, and Death* (A Series of Books in Psychology). New York, NY: WH Freeman/ Times Books/Henry Holt & Co; 1975.

[20] Church RM. The varied effects of punishment on behaviour. *Psychological Review.* 1963;70(5):369.
Church RM. Response suppression. *Punishment and Aversive Behaviour* New York: Appleton-Century-Crofts. 1969:111–156.

[21] Ferster CB, Skinner BF. *Schedules of Reinforcement.* East Norwalk, CT, US: Appleton-Century-Crofts; 1957.

[22] Bornstein MH, Benasich AA. Infant habituation: Assessments of individual differences and short-term reliability at five months. *Child Development.* 1986;57(1):87–99.

[23] Colombo J, Mitchell DW. Infant visual habituation. *Neurobiology of Learning and Memory.* 2009;92(2):225–234.

[24] Pavlov IP. *Conditioned Reflexes: An Investigation of the Physiological Activity of the Cerebral Cortex.* Oxford, England: Oxford University Press; 1927.

[25] Watson JB. Psychology as the behaviourist views it. *Psychological Review.* 1913;20(2):158-177.
Watson JB. *Psychology from the Standpoint of a Behaviourist.* Philadelphia, PA: J. B. Lippincott Company; 1919.

[26] Watson JB, Rayner R. Conditioned emotional responses. *Journal of Experimental Psychology.* 1920;3(1):1–14.

[27] Bregman EO. An attempt to modify the emotional attitudes of infants by the conditioned response technique. *The Pedagogical Seminary and Journal of Genetic Psychology.* 1934;45:169–198.

[28] Garcia J, Ervin F. Gustatory-visceral and telereceptor-cutaneous conditioning: Adaptation in internal and external milieus. *Communications in Behavioural Biology.* 1968;1(Part A):389–415.

[29] Bandura, A., Ross, D., & Ross, S. A. (1961). Transmission of aggression through imitation of aggressive models. *Journal of Abnormal and Social Psychology,* 63, 575–582.

Bandura, A., Ross, D., & Ross, S. A. (1963). Imitation of film-mediated aggressive models. *Journal of Abnormal and Social Psychology*, 66, 3–11. Bandura, A. (1965). Influence of models' reinforcement contingencies on the acquisition of imitative responses. *Journal of Personality and Social Psychology*, 1(6), 589–595.

[30] Cahill, L., Haier, R. J., Fallon, J., Alkire, M. T., Tang, C., Keator, D., Wu, J., & McGaugh, J. L. (1996). Amygdala activity at encoding correlated with long-term, free recall of emotional information. *Proceedings of the National Academy of Sciences of the United States of America*, 93(15), 8016–8021. https://doi.org/10.1073/pnas.93.15.8016

[31] Kapleau P. *The Wheel of Death: Writings from Zen Buddhist and other Sources* New York: Harper & Row; 1971, p. 25.

[32] Warren, R. M., & Warren, R. P. (1970). Auditory illusions and confusions. *Scientific American*, 223(6), 30–37.

[33] Shun'ei T. *Living Yogacara*. Boston: Wisdom Publications; 2009.

[34] Trungpa C. *Karma seminar*. Halifax, Nova Scotia: Vajradhatu Publications; 1972, p. 16.

[35] Atsma AJ. Moirai. 2017; http://www.theoi.com/Daimon/Moirai.html. Accessed March 13, 2018.

[36] Homer. *The Iliad*. Chicago, IL: University of Chicago Press; 1951, 20, 125–128.

[37] Even this story, however, doesn't say we have entirely no choice. Achilles' mother, Thetis, gave him the prophecy that he could live in obscurity and die an old man, or he could choose to fight in the Trojan war, die young, and have an immortal reputation. Achilles chose how to act (karma), which then resulted in a specific fated consequence.

[38] Trungpa C. Karma seminar. Halifax, Nova Scotia: Vajradhatu Publications; 1972, p. 23.

[39] Kapleau P. *The Wheel of Death: Writings from Zen Buddhist and other Sources* New York: Harper & Row; 1971, p. 27.

[40] Kyabgon T. *Karma: What It Is, What It Isn't, Why It Matters.* Boston, MA: Shambhala; 2015.

[41] Kapleau P. *The Wheel of Death: Writings from Zen Buddhist and other Sources* New York: Harper & Row; 1971, p. 20.

[42] This focus on intention being crucial to the creation of karma was a radical departure from the way it was typically understood at the time of the Buddha. '... the Buddha understood karma in quite a different sense from that of his compatriots, and that different sense was soteriologically relevant. In the Brahmanical context, karma is significant *ritual* action, or (by the time of the early Upaniṣads) actual good and bad *deeds* (the implication being that a bad intention without a bad deed does not count). For Jains (as an example of another renouncer group for whom we have some information), karma was seen as quasi-material, like a polluting dirt which weighed down the Self and kept it in saṃsāra. Thus, for Jains, all karma is one way or another bad. Ultimately, one should cease acting altogether. The Buddha's position was quite different from either of these groups and (as with his position on the Self) it was different as far as we can tell from all others in India. It was the Buddha who declared that karma is intention, a mental event. In so doing, Gombrich comments, the Buddha 'turned the Brahmin ideology upside down and ethicized the universe. I do not see how one could exaggerate the importance of the Buddha's ethicisation of the world, which I regard as a turning point in the history of civilization.' (Williams P, Tribe A, Wynne A. *Buddhist Thought: A complete introduction to the Indian tradition.* 2nd Ed ed. London: Routledge; 2012, pp. 53-54).

[43] McDermott JP. *Development in the early Buddhist concept of kamma/karma.* New Delhi, India: Munshiram Manoharlal Publishers; 1984, p. 26.

[44] Drepung Gomang Monastery. The Four Foundations: thoughts which turn the mind towards the dharma. 2012; http://drepunggomang.org/dharma-topics/123-the-four-foundations-thoughts-which-turn-the-mind-towards-the-dharma.   Accessed 2018, March 19.

45 Kyabgon T. *Karma: What It Is, What It Isn't, Why It Matters.* Boston, MA: Shambhala; 2015, pp. 52–53.

46 Kapleau P. *The Wheel of Death: Writings from Zen Buddhist and other Sources* New York: Harper & Row; 1971, pp. 25–26.

47 Bhikkhu T. Upajjhatthana Sutta: Subjects for Contemplation (AN 5.57). 1997; https://www.accesstoinsight.org/tipitaka/an/an05/an05.057.than.html. Accessed March 20, 2018.

48 Trungpa C. *Karma seminar.* Halifax, Nova Scotia: Vajradhatu Publications; 1972, p. 30.

49 Latané B, Darley JM. Group inhibition of bystander intervention in emergencies. *Journal of Personality and Social Psychology.* 1968;10:215–221.

50 Kyabgon T. *Karma: What It Is, What It Isn't, Why It Matters.* Boston, MA: Shambhala; 2015, p. 40.

51 Bhikkhu T. Sakalika Sutta: The Stone Silver (SN 1.38). 1999; https://www.accesstoinsight.org/ati/tipitaka/sn/sn01/sn01.038.than.html. Accessed March 21, 2018.

52 Bhikkhu T. Sakalika Sutta: The Stone Silver (SN 4.13). 1999; https://www.accesstoinsight.org/ati/tipitaka/sn/sn04/sn04.013.than.html. Accessed March 21, 2018.

53 McDermott JP. *Development in the early Buddhist concept of kamma/karma.* New Delhi, India: Munshiram Manoharlal Publishers; 1984, pp. 108–109.

54 Deshimaru T. *Zen & karma.* Chino Valley, Arizona: Hohm Press; 2016, p. 83.

55 Deshimaru T. *Zen & karma.* Chino Valley, Arizona: Hohm Press; 2016, p. 84.

56 McDermott JP. *Development in the early Buddhist concept of kamma/karma.* New Delhi, India: Munshiram Manoharlal Publishers; 1984, p. 151.

[57] Feeney JA, Noller P. Attachment style as a predictor of adult romantic relationships. *Journal of Personality and Social Psychology*. 1990;58(2):281–291.

Simpson JA, Collins WA, Tran S, Haydon KC. Attachment and the experience and expression of emotions in romantic relationships: A developmental perspective. *Journal of Personality and Social Psychology*. 2007;92(2):355–367.

[58] The Strange Situation has also been conducted with fathers and other caregivers, and these studies show the same basic results. I discuss it with relevance to mothers, simply because the majority of research has been conducted with mothers and their babies as the participants.

[59] Returning to the idea of karmic seeds being able to be transmitted from one life to another, there is a way we see this in empirical science. Children who grew up with a particular attachment style tend to parent their children in a way that leads to their children having the same attachment style. In this way, it seems the karmic seeds can ripen in future lifetimes. (Main M, Hesse E. Parents' unresolved traumatic experiences are related to infant disorganized attachment status: Is frightened and/or frightening parental behaviour the linking mechanism? In: Greenberg MT, Cicchetti D, Cummings EM, eds. *The John D. and Catherine T. MacArthur Foundation series on mental health and development. Attachment in the preschool years: Theory, research, and intervention*. Chicago, IL: University of Chicago Press; 1990:161–182.)

[60] Sarkissian H, Chatterjee A, De Brigard F, Knobe J, Nichols S, Sirker S. Is Belief in Free Will a Cultural Universal? *Mind & Language*. 2010;25(3):346–358.

[61] Bargh JA, Chen M, Burrows L. Automaticity of social behaviour: Direct effects of trait construct and stereotype activation on action. *Journal of Personality and Social Psychology*. 1996;71(2):230–244.

[62] Milgram S. Behavioural Study of obedience. *The Journal of Abnormal and Social Psychology*. 1963;67(4):371–378.

63 Wegner DM, Wheatley T. Apparent mental causation: Sources of the experience of will. *American Psychologist.* 1999;54(7):480–492.

64 Wegner DM, Sparrow B, Winerman L. Vicarious Agency: Experiencing Control Over the Movements of Others. *Journal of Personality and Social Psychology.* 2004;86(6):838–848.

65 Wegner DM, Sparrow B, Winerman L. Vicarious Agency: Experiencing Control Over the Movements of Others. *Journal of Personality and Social Psychology.* 2004;86(6):838–848.

66 Cannon WB. 'Voodoo' death. *American Anthropologist.* 1942;44(2): 169–181.

67 Pronin E, Wegner DM, McCarthy K, Rodriguez S. Everyday magical powers: The role of apparent mental causation in the overestimation of personal influence. *Journal of Personality and Social Psychology.* 2006;91(2):218–231.

68 Wegner DM, Wheatley T. Apparent mental causation: Sources of the experience of will. American Psychologist. 1999;54(7):480-492

69 Wheatley T. *When unintentional acts feel intentional: The power of an illusory purpose.* Department of Psychology, University of Virginia; 2001, p. 25.

70 Wheatley T. *When unintentional acts feel intentional: The power of an illusory purpose.* Department of Psychology, University of Virginia; 2001, p. 29.

71 Kornhuber HH, Deecke L. Hirnpotentialänderungen bei Willkürbewegungen und passiven Bewegungen des Menschen: Bereitschaftspotential und reafferente Potentiale. *Pflüger's Archiv für die gesamte Physiologie des Menschen und der Tiere.* 1965;284:1-17.

72 Libet B. Unconscious cerebral initiative and the role of conscious will in voluntary action. *Behavioural and Brain Sciences.* 1985;8:529–539. Libet B, Gleason CA, Wright EW, Pearl DK. Time of conscious intention to act in relation to onset of cerebral activity (readiness-potential): The unconscious initiation of a freely voluntary act. *Brain.* 1983;106(3):623–642.

[73] Wegner DM, Wheatley T. Apparent mental causation: Sources of the experience of will. *American Psychologist*. 1999;54(7):480–492, pp.482, 489–490.

[74] Boswell, J. (1791/1986). *The Life of Samuel Johnson*. New York: Penguin Books.

[75] Skinner, B. F. (c. 1972). Operant Conditioning video interview. Retrieved from https://youtu.be/I_ctJqjlrHA

[76] Palahniuk C. *Lullaby*. New York: Anchor Books; 2003, p. 20.

[77] Waddington CH. *The strategy of the genes. A discussion of some aspects of theoretical biology. With an appendix by H. Kacser.* London: George Allen & Unwin, Ltd.; 1957.

[78] Waddington designed this analogy to describe cellular differentiation in the brain, but it is also useful for considering the development of a person.

[79] Waddington CH. Canalization of development and the inheritance of acquired characters. *Nature*. 1942;150:563.

[80] See, for example, the *Maha-Nidana Sutta and the Paticca-samuppada-vibhanga Sutta* if you would like to read some of the original ways it was described.
- Bhikkhu T. Maha-nidana sutta: The great causes discourse. 1997; BCBS:https://www.accesstoinsight.org/tipitaka/dn/dn.15.0.than.html. Accessed June 30, 2018.
- Bhikkhu T. Paticca-samuppada-vibhanga sutta: Analysis of dependent co-arising (SN 12.2). 1997; BCBS Edition:https://www.accesstoinsight.org/tipitaka/sn/sn12/sn12.002.than.html. Accessed June 30, 2018.

[81] Trungpa C. *Karma and the Twelve Nidanas*. Halifax, Nova Scotia: Vajradhatu Publication; 1972, p. 6.

[82] If you're keeping scores on your lucky Buddhist jargon scorecard, it is at this level that the possibility for the five skandhas arise, with the one material skandha and four mental skandhas.

[83] Ray R. *Indestructible Truth*. Boston, MA: Shambhala; 2002.

[84] For the really geeky, Buddhaghosa's commentary on the Abhidharma Pitaka describes a difference between inoperative consciousness and resultant consciousness that may be instructive. As described in the Twelve Nidanas, we have six sense doors, and when they come into contact with an appropriate object for that sense, consciousness arises. This arising is karmically inoperative. It does not cause intentions, planning, or action on its own. Only once we move past what we see, taste, hear, touch, and smell to wanting some and rejecting others do we create karma.

'Inoperative consciousness,' as Buddhaghosa explains, 'it can be best clarified by the following illustration. Suppose a person walks into a room in which he has never been before. As he steps into that room, there is the briefest instant when he is aware of his surroundings as a whole, before he has begun to discriminate between individual objects in the room, before he sees tables, chairs, people, etc. as such. His consciousness during this moment, before his mind begins to evaluate his surroundings, is termed inoperative consciousness.' Thus, to paraphrase Buddhaghosa's explanation, inoperative consciousness is that which arises prior to emotional or evaluative discrimination, yet sets the life-continuum in motion in the sense that it exists behind all subsequent mental states. In this sense, it must be considered non-volitional. For this reason, it too is non-effective, being the cause of no further results. (McDermott JP. Development in the early Buddhist concept of kamma/karma. New Delhi, India: Munshiram Manoharlal Publishers; 1984, p. 81)

[85] Jarudi I, Kreps T, Bloom P. Is a refrigerator good or evil? The moral evaluation of everyday objects. *Social Justice Research*. 2008;21:457-469.

[86] Ray R. *Indestructible Truth*. Boston, MA: Shambhala; 2002, p.381.

[87] Ray R. *Indestructible Truth*. Boston, MA: Shambhala; 2002, p.382.

[88] Trungpa C. *Karma seminar*. Halifax, Nova Scotia: Vajradhatu Publications; 1972, p. 27.

[89] Kyabgon T. *Karma: What It Is, What It Isn't, Why It Matters*. Boston, MA: Shambhala; 2015, p. 73.

[90] Trungpa C. *Karma seminar*. Halifax, Nova Scotia: Vajradhatu Publications; 1972, p. 52.

[91] Trungpa C. *Karma seminar*. Halifax, Nova Scotia: Vajradhatu Publications; 1972, pp. 18–19.

[92] Deshimaru T. *Zen & karma*. Chino Valley, Arizona: Hohm Press; 2016, p. 22.

[93] McDermott JP. *Development in the early Buddhist concept of kamma/ karma*. New Delhi, India: Munshiram Manoharlal Publishers; 1984, p. 23.